HOW TO BECOME SMARTER WHILE ENTERTAINING YOURSELF

# Human Lines

## Gazmend Ceno

# CONTENTS

Introduction
V

List of Puzzles
XVII

Puzzles
1

Solutions
75

# INTRODUCTION

**Albcell in a nutshell:** Albcell is composed of a 10 x 10 grid of alternating diamonds and circles. Each puzzle is divided into a number of cell groups, separated by thick lines. Can you place the numbers between 0 and 9 *once* in each row, column and cell group, putting the odd numbers (1, 3, 5, 7, 9) into the diamonds, and the even numbers (0, 2, 4, 6, 8) into the circles?

In the following pages we'll solve an example Albcell puzzle together. To keep things simple, we'll work out the odd and even numbers separately. Once you're more familiar with the process, you can always mix and match odd and even to your taste, which should make the puzzles more fun to do. Now let's try one …

## Cell Groups

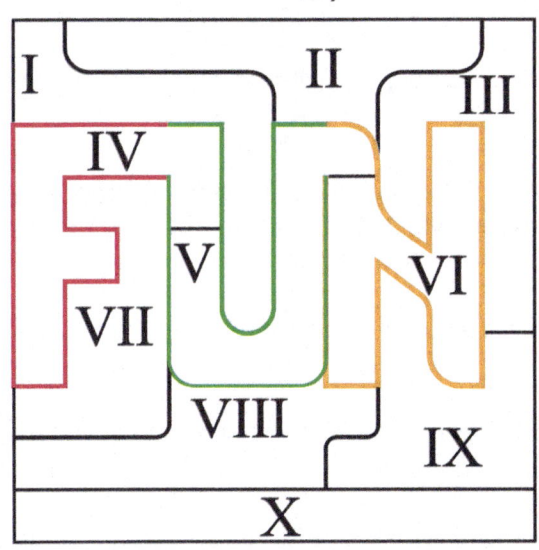

Look at the first diagram. It contains Roman numerals that identify the 10 cell groups in this particular puzzle. Each group contains 10 cells. If you're wondering where these cells are, look at diagram 2, which shows the starting grid for the puzzle. Circles contain even numbers; diamonds contain odd numbers. For ease of reference, I've also given each column a letter and each row a number. (This is just to make the solution easier to follow – the actual puzzles don't have this notation).

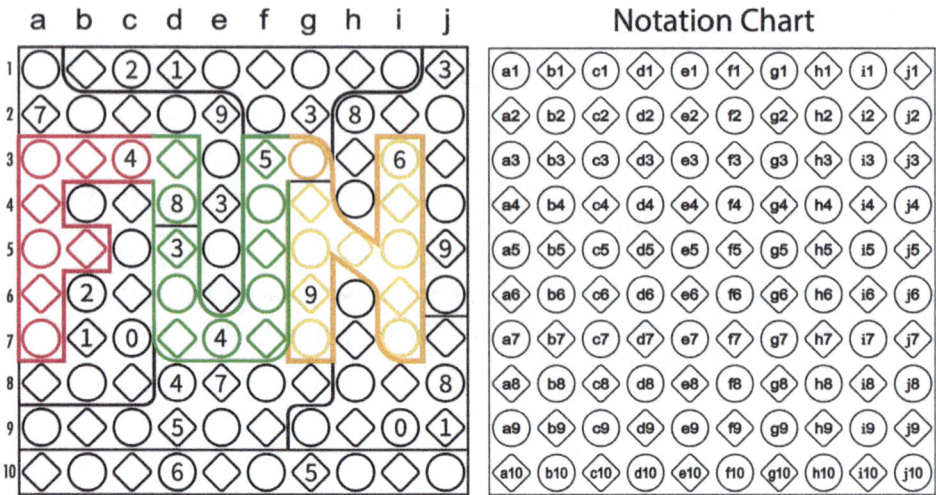

In the third diagram (the *Notation Chart*), you can pinpoint the location of any particular cell according to its corresponding column and row. Keep in mind that although each puzzle contains a different picture and a different ordering of numbers, the underlying cell structure is always the same from one puzzle to the next.

Now that you've got the essentials, grab a pencil and let's look at the puzzle itself. At this point it's worth repeating the basic rule:

**Place the numbers between 0 and 9 *once* in each row, column and cell group, putting the odd numbers (1, 3, 5, 7, 9) into the diamonds, and the even numbers (0, 2, 4, 6, 8) into the circles.**

(Remember, a number can be used only *once* in each row, column and cell group.)

At first the puzzle may seem daunting – but there are a few techniques you can use to solve it. Let's start from the beginning…

Use the diagram on the next page as a worksheet on which to keep track of your progress, by adding numbers until the puzzle is completed.

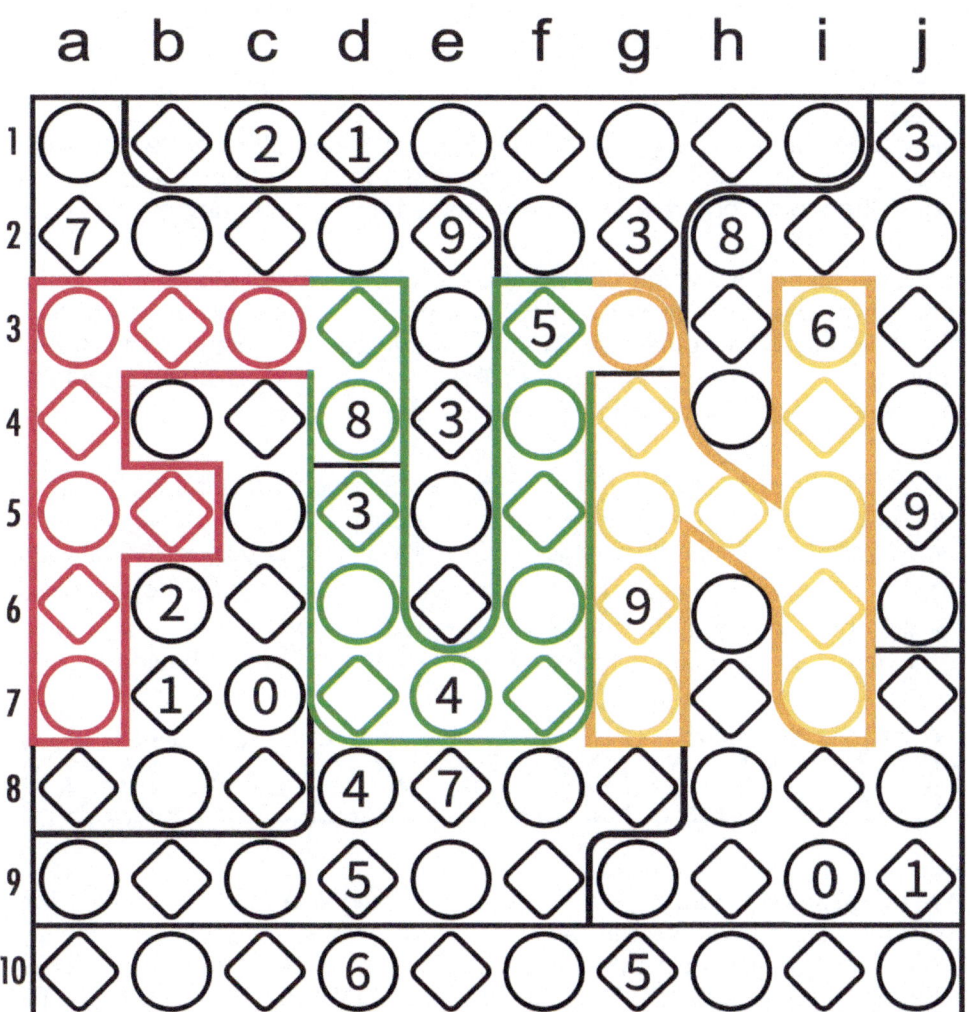

VII

**Odd numbers**

First, look at the odd numbers in the last column, **j**. 1, 3 and 9 are given, but we still need 5 and 7. Luckily for us, there is already a 5 in group V, cell *f3*, which means there can't be a 5 in *j3*.[1] This leaves 7 as the only possible candidate for that cell. This also enables us to fill in the last diamond in column **j**, *j7*, with the number 5. So grab your pencil and fill in cells *j3*(7) and *j7*(5).

Next, add the remaining odd numbers in cell group III, since by the same logic 5 can only be in *i2* and the remaining 1 in *h3*. This then allows us to complete the second row by filling in the remaining odd number (1) in *c2*.

With me so far? Now you can practice what you've learned by completing column **g**. Use the number 7 in *e8* as a guide. This will allow you to fill in the cells at *g4* and *g8* easily. Then, to reinforce what we've just learned, look at what's missing in column **e**. Thanks to the 5 in *g10*, you should be able to see that 1 belongs in *e10* and 5 in *e6*.

Once you've done that, try to identify the missing odd numbers in group VIII, in cells *b9* and *f9*. Since there is no way to be sure just yet which is which, mark both candidates lightly in the cells, as shown in the diagram below. You don't have to do this, of course – if you prefer you could always "write" them in your memory. Whichever method you choose, our ultimate goal here is to "complete" the row for the single purpose of finding *h9*.

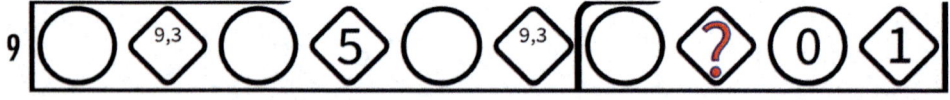

We're making progress. Now we can consider a new approach that becomes clear if we look at cell *i10*. At first glance, it seems that this cell could contain any odd number except 5 and 1. But if you look closely enough, there is a catch! You should notice that the 7 in *g4* covers off *i4*

---

[1] Why can't we have a 5 there? Because then the third row would have two 5s, and that would be illegal. We can't bend the rules here, since our puzzle is based on math, not politics!

and *i6*, and there's no way it can be in *i8*. So we can say with certainty that in column **i** there is no other home for the 7 except *i10*.

Next, focus on the two number 3s in cells *d5* and *e4*. Draw two imaginary arrows toward cell group VI, so that they line up with the two diamonds in that group, *h5* and *i4*. Can you see now why the number 3 in group VI can only go in *i6*?

This last discovery also enables us to fill in *h7* and *i8 in* group IX.

Look upwards at the first number we found, the 7 in *j3*. Where do you think the 7 in column **d** can go, since *d3* is now unavailable? Next, by combining imaginary lines from *j3* (horizontal) and *a2* (vertical), can you deduce where the 7 is located in group IV? If you said *b5* you were correct! This also helps us to complete column **d** (*d3* being the last odd number remaining in that column), and then the third row.

From here we can resolve the uncertainty around cells *b9* and *f9*. Thanks to the number 3 that we've just placed in the third row, in *b3*, we can now deduce both numbers as 9*(b9)* and 3*(f9)*.

We can then finish column **b** by adding the remaining 5 in *b1*. While we're here, let's remain at the top a little longer, and fill in *f1* and *h1*. (To do this, refer to the 7 in *h9*). Once you've completed that, add the last number in column **h**. Now we're certainly making some serious progress!

This is how our Albcell puzzle should now look:

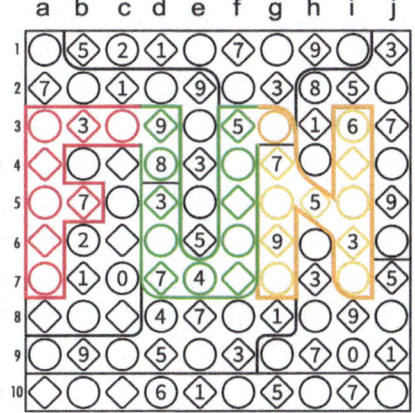

*(Hopefully your version looks the same! If it doesn't, retrace your steps and try to figure out where you went wrong.)*

Next, follow these steps:
1. Complete group VI by adding 1 at *i4*.
2. With the help of the 9 in *j5*, and the 1 in *b7*, you should be able to complete column **f**.
3. In which cells do you think the 1 and 7 in row 6 can go? They must be *a6* and *c6*, of course – and the positions relate directly to the numbers in *a2* and *c2*.

Continue with the missing odd number in group IV. Finding this should help us finish row 4. From here the only odd numbers still missing are the four digits in the bottom-left corner. Hopefully you shouldn't need any help to find them by yourself ...

**Even numbers**

Now let's focus on the even numbers. Look at *d6* in the diagram on the right, in which I have included all the odd numbers we've found so far.

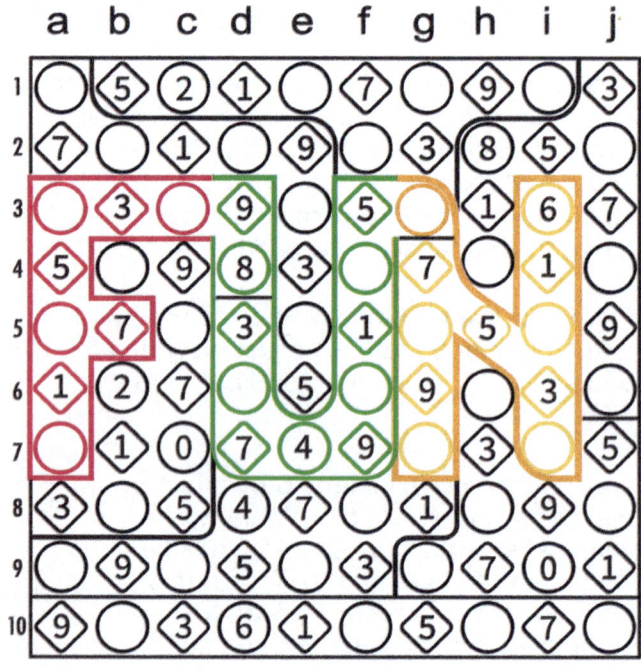

Cell *d6* is empty, but the surrounding cells provide lots of hints as to what it might contain! The numbers 8(*d4*), 2(*b6*) and 6(*d10*) all "cross" at cell *d6*, which means that *d6* cannot contain any of them. How about the remaining even numbers, 0 and 4? But wait!

x

Doesn't group V already have a 4? This tells us that *d6* can only contain a 0.

Now look at the 0 in *i9*. By applying the elimination technique we used before, we can deduce what's missing in *f8*. (The question mark can only be 0, because group VIII still needs a 0, and the ninth row can't have a second one!)

Now look at 2*(c1)*, 0*(c7)*, 6*(i3)* and 8*(d4)*. Can you find the number in *c3* in group IV based on this information? Great! Let's remain with group IV a little longer. Although we only know two of the five even numbers required to complete the group, we can clarify the picture a little further by penciling in the missing numbers in all their probable cells.

Look at the vertical diagram. You'll notice that in this particular case, the positions of 0, 2 and 6 in group IV are all in column **a**. Because of this, we can safely assume that cells *a1* and *a9* must contain either 4

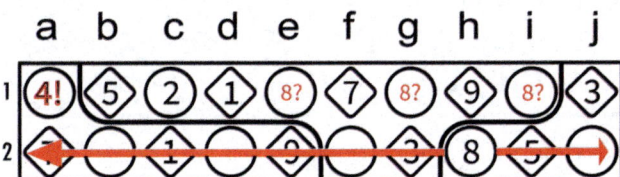

or 8. Although it's not clear immediately which is which, as you focus more on the puzzle, you might see that the number 8 in column **h** covers off *f2*. This means that the 8 in cell group II can only be located somewhere in the first row. So we can safely assume that *a1* must be 4! And because we now know that *a9* is 8, this gives us another 8 in *c5*! We can also guess what *j8* is, with the help of *h2*, since these two numbers make it clear where the 8 in group IX must be. This, in turn, gives us the number 8 in group V *(f6)*. Why? Because both *j6* and *h6* are covered off. If you mark 4 and 6 in *b4* and *b8* respectively, the other two missing

numbers in column **b** can be found straight away. So far, your puzzle should look like this:

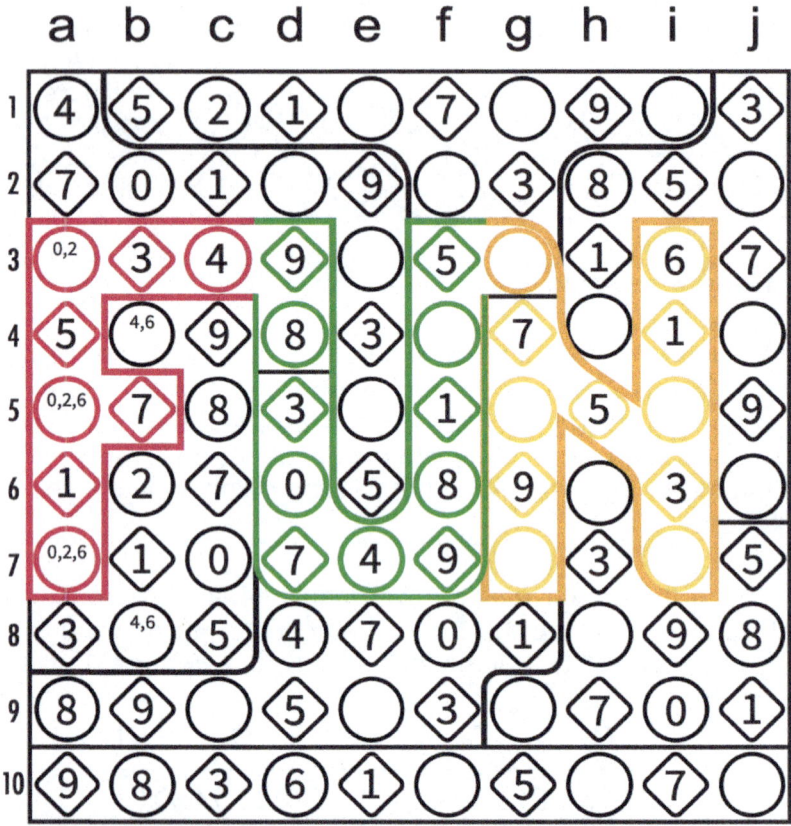

Now complete the following steps:
1. Find *f2* using *a1*. (Where else can 4 find a home in group II?)
2. Next deduce *f10*. It should be easy, since we can cross-reference the even numbers we have in column **f** (4, 8, 0) and row 10 (8, 6). In other words, since none of those numbers can be in *f10*, it must contain a 2. This step enables us to complete group V and column **b** *(see figure below)*.

XII

Write 4 and 6 in *b4* and *b8* respectively, then complete the eighth row.

3. Next, consider all the circles we filled with multiple candidates in group IV. Now that we've solved group V, the number 2 in *g3* should help us complete the third row. Then we can fill in the missing numbers (2, 6) in group I by first completing column *d*. Then, with the help of 6 in *e5*, we can figure out *a5* and *a7*.

This is how the puzzle should look now:

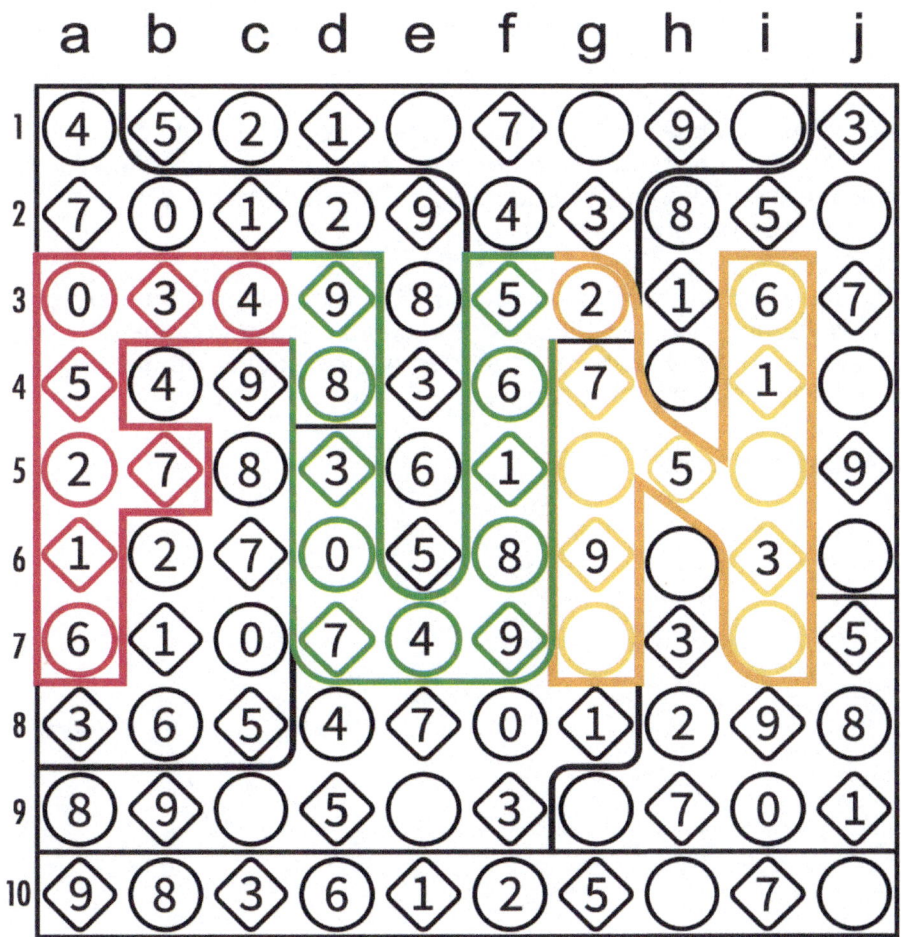

Take a deep breath. We're almost there!

Now, having worked out most of the numbers in column **c**, we can add *c9* and then complete group VIII by adding a 2 to *e9*. This comes in handy for completing both the ninth row and column **e**! Next, add the last number in group IX. (I'm talking about the 6 in *h6,* of course.) After that, let's keep things interesting and take a look at the letter N of the word 'FUN'. This remains the main unexplored area, which we can complete using our newly acquired skills. Of course, we can approach this problem from many angles – that's the advantage of having accumulated so much data!

For example, you could draw an imaginary line along the fifth row, and use the 2, 6 and 8 there, together with the 4 and 0 in group IX, to find *g5* and *i5*.

Then, by making use of the position of the 2 in *g3*, you could deduce *g7* (8) and *i7* (2). From here, finishing columns **g** and **i** is a mere formality. Now add a 6 to the end of the second row *(j2)*. Then refer to the 2 in h8 to figure out why *h4* can only contain a 0.

What you do from here is up to you! The remaining four empty circles could be deduced in several ways. You could choose to continue with the 2 or the 4 in group III (where we started our adventure with the lucky 7 in *j3*), or in the tenth row, by adding 4 and 0.

Either way, well done!

*The Author*

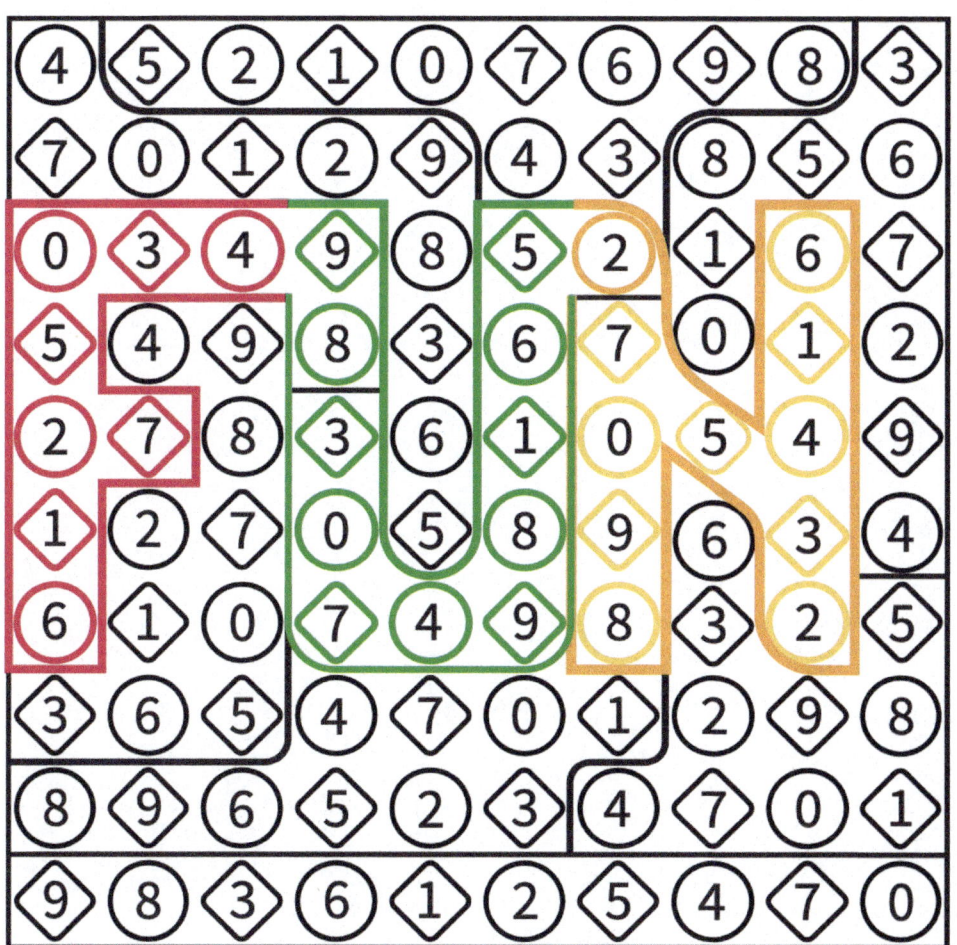

# List of Puzzles

1.
2.
3.
4.
5.
6.
7.
8.
9.
10. Amantium irae amoris integratio est
11.
12. Opal and Ruby Jewlery
13.
14.
15.
16. Archeological Finds
17.
18.
19.
20. Queen of Spades
21. The Sign
22.
23. Astral Projection & The Dreaming Body
24.
25.
26.
27.
28.
29.
30.
31. The View From Above
32. In Gossip Mode
33.
34. The Real Question
35.
36. Synergy
37. The Arguments
38.
39.
40. The Man with the Halo
41. Staring into the Abyss
42.
43.
44.
45. A Man and a Woman
46.
47. The Scream
48. Jigsaw Pieces
49. The Sphinx
50.
51. Inside Zeus' Temple
52.
53.
54. Imressions of Africa
55. The Shadow Deal
56.
57.
58. The Apprasial
59.
60.
61.
62.
63.
64.
65. The Vision
66.
67.
68.
69.
70.
71. The Crime Scene
72..
73..
74.

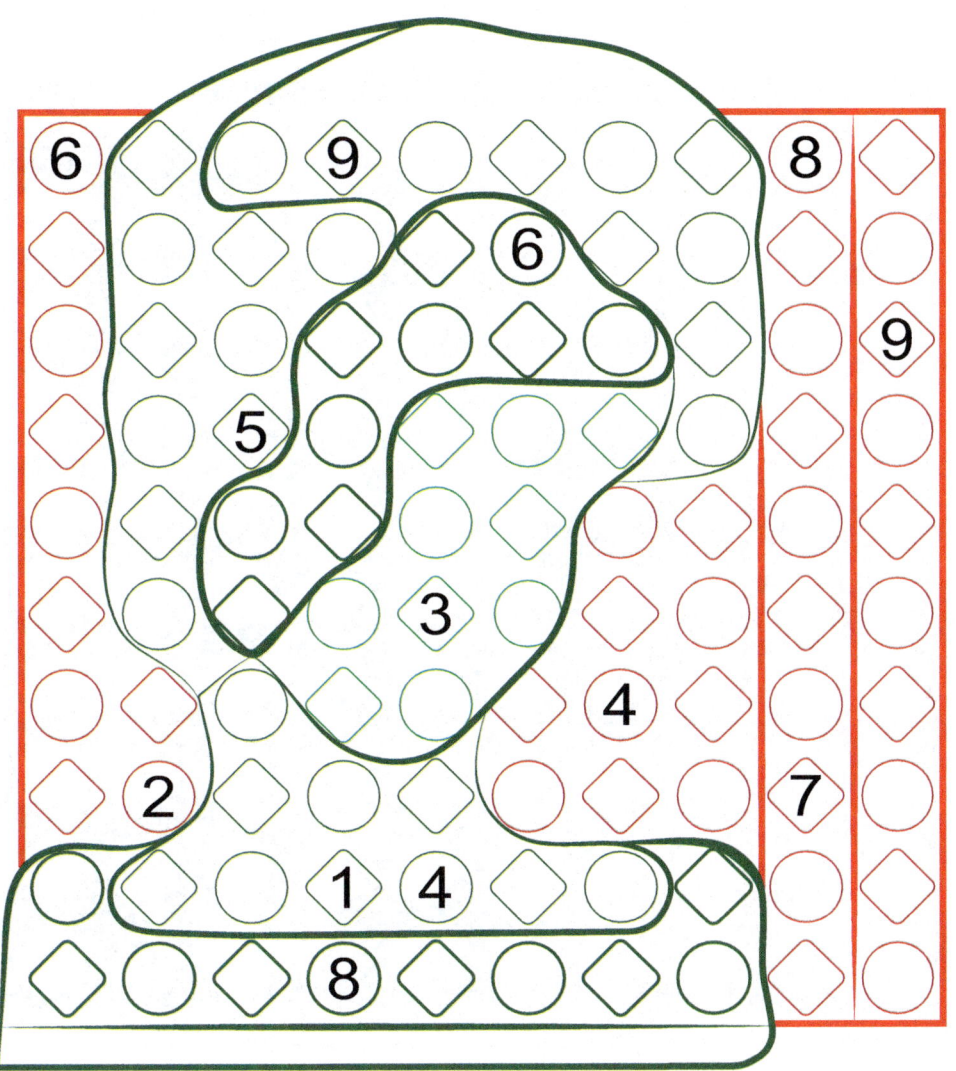

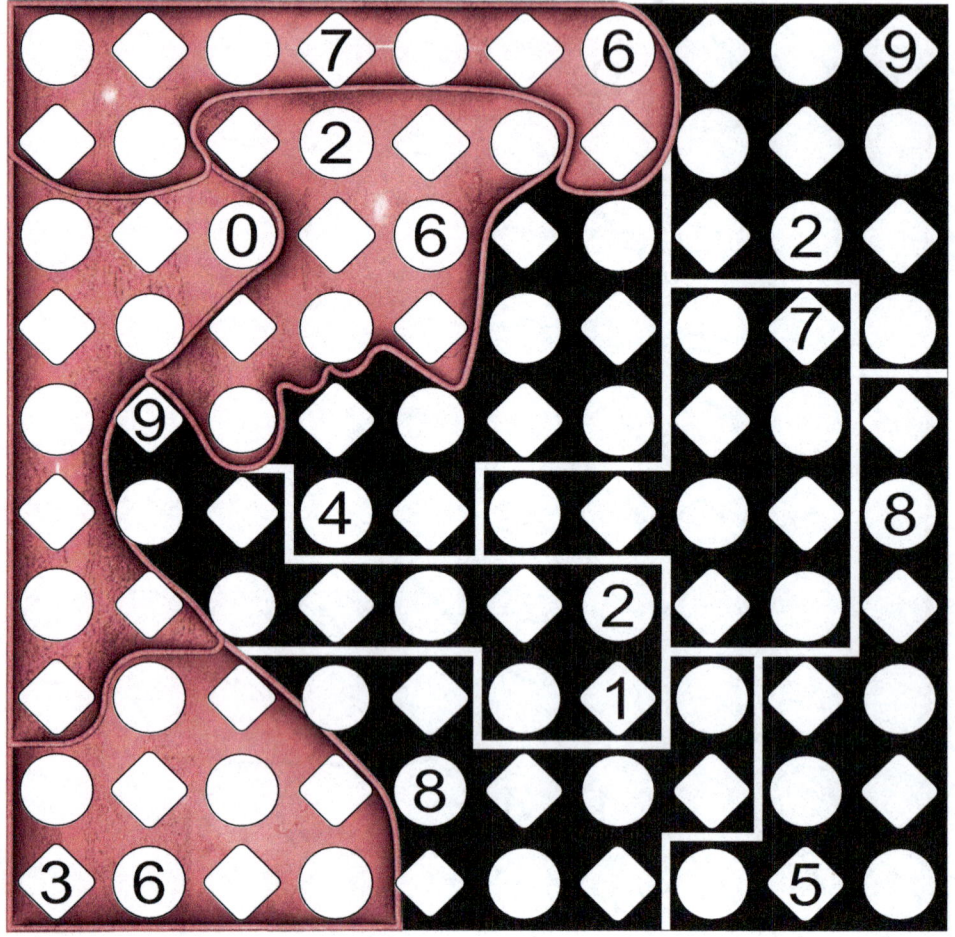

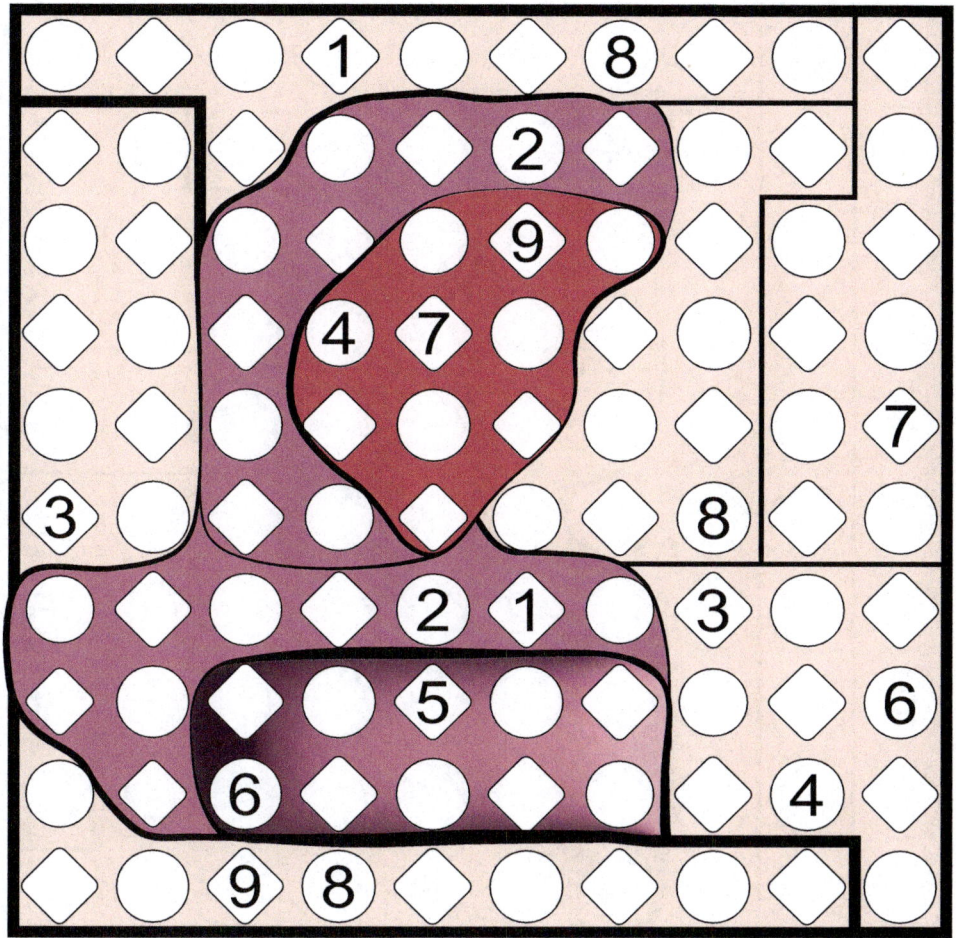

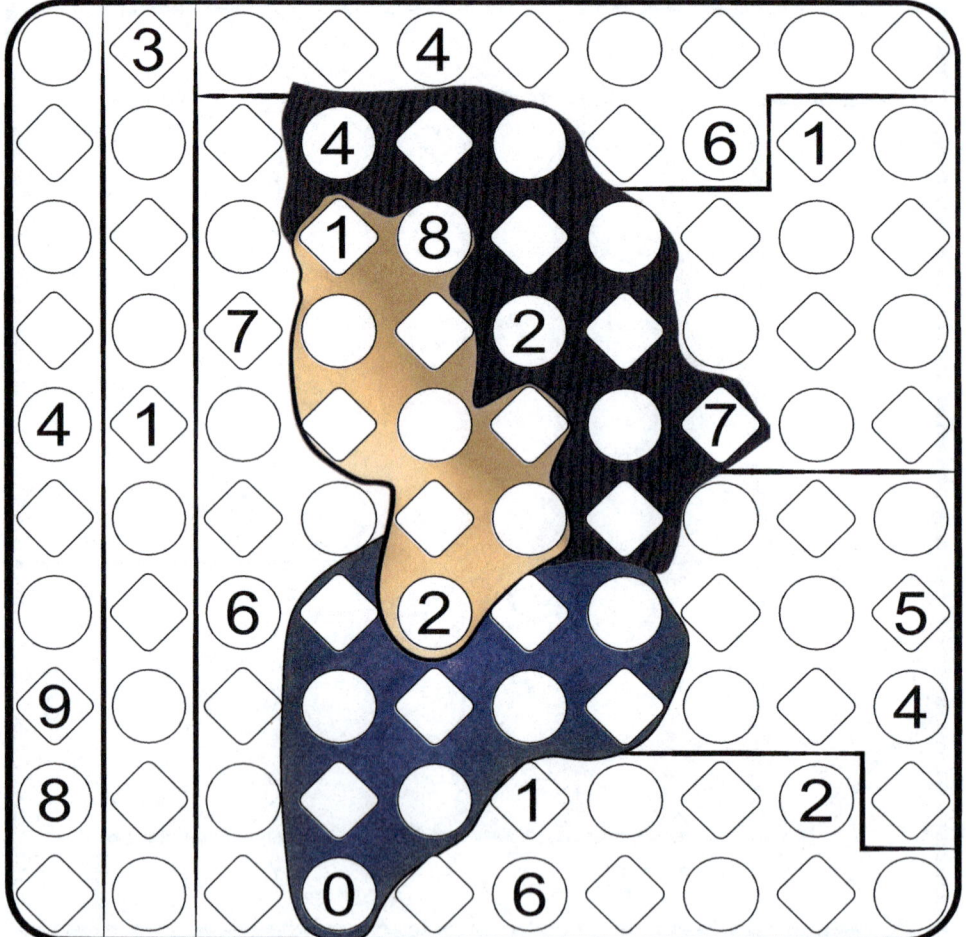

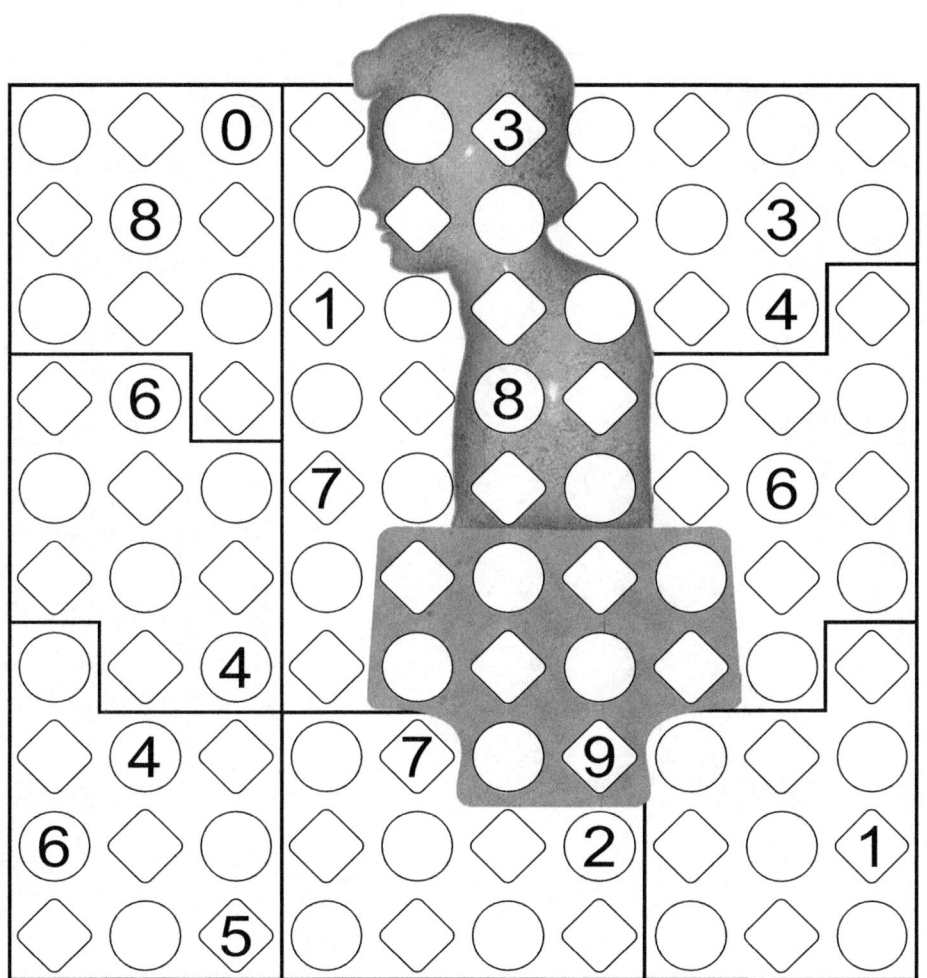

5

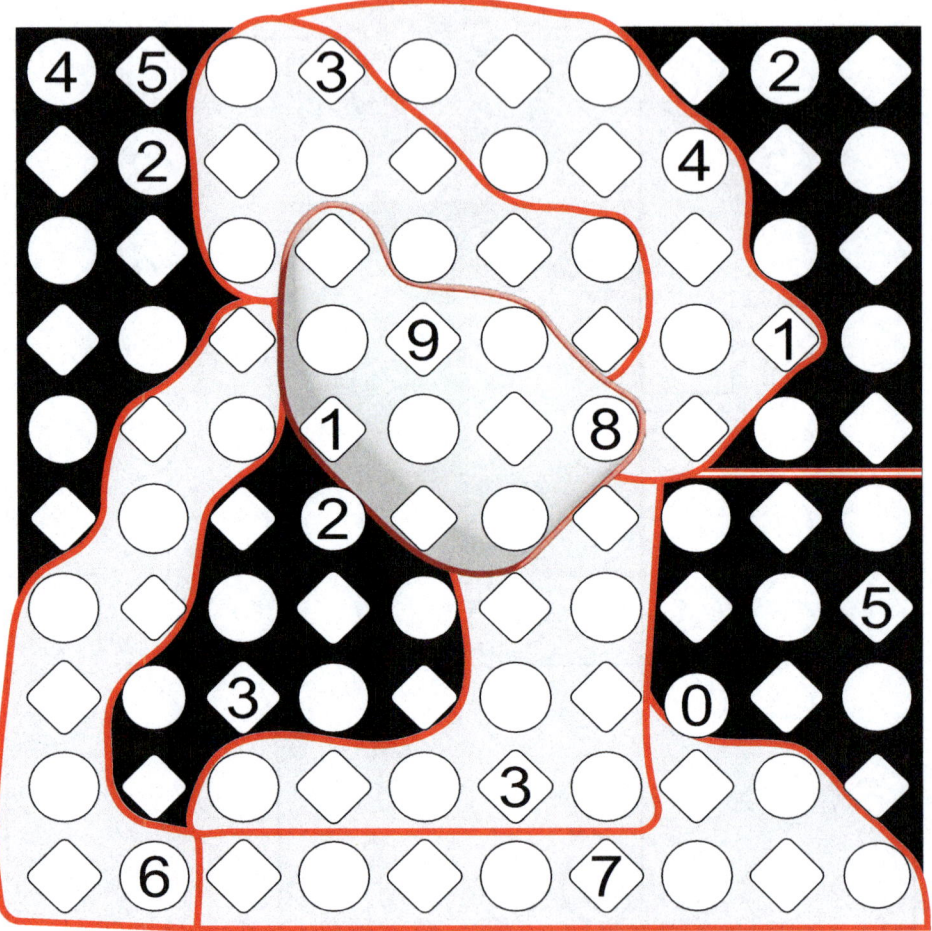

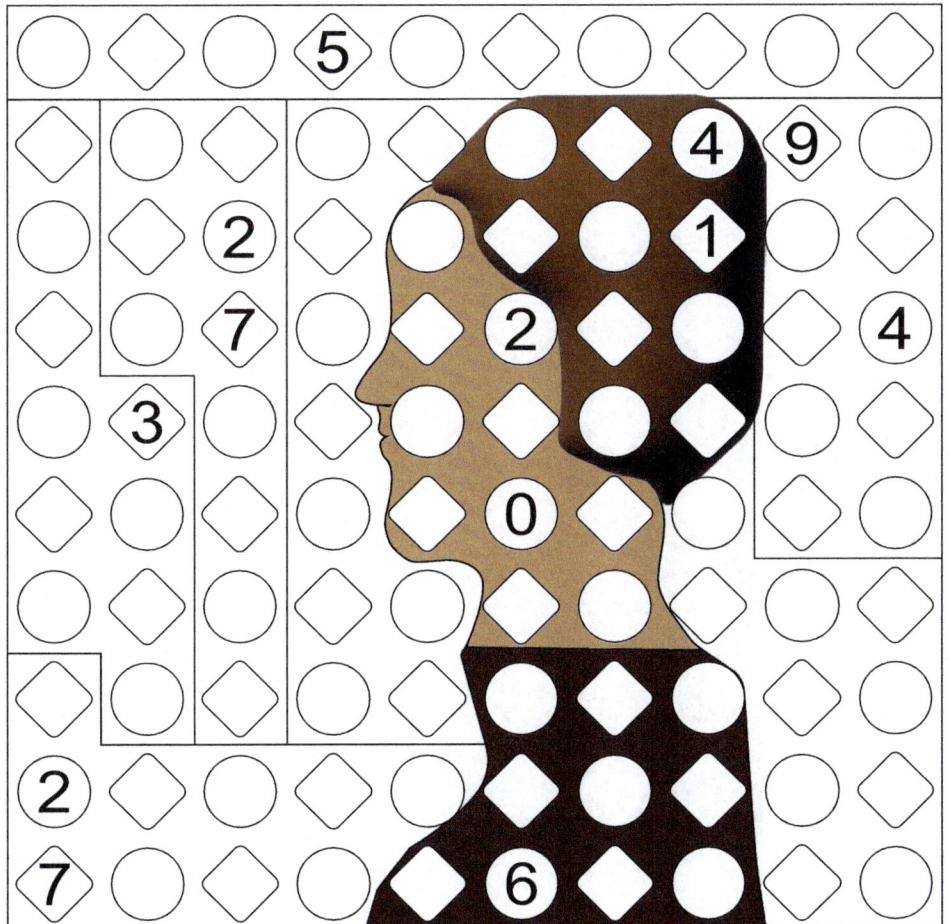

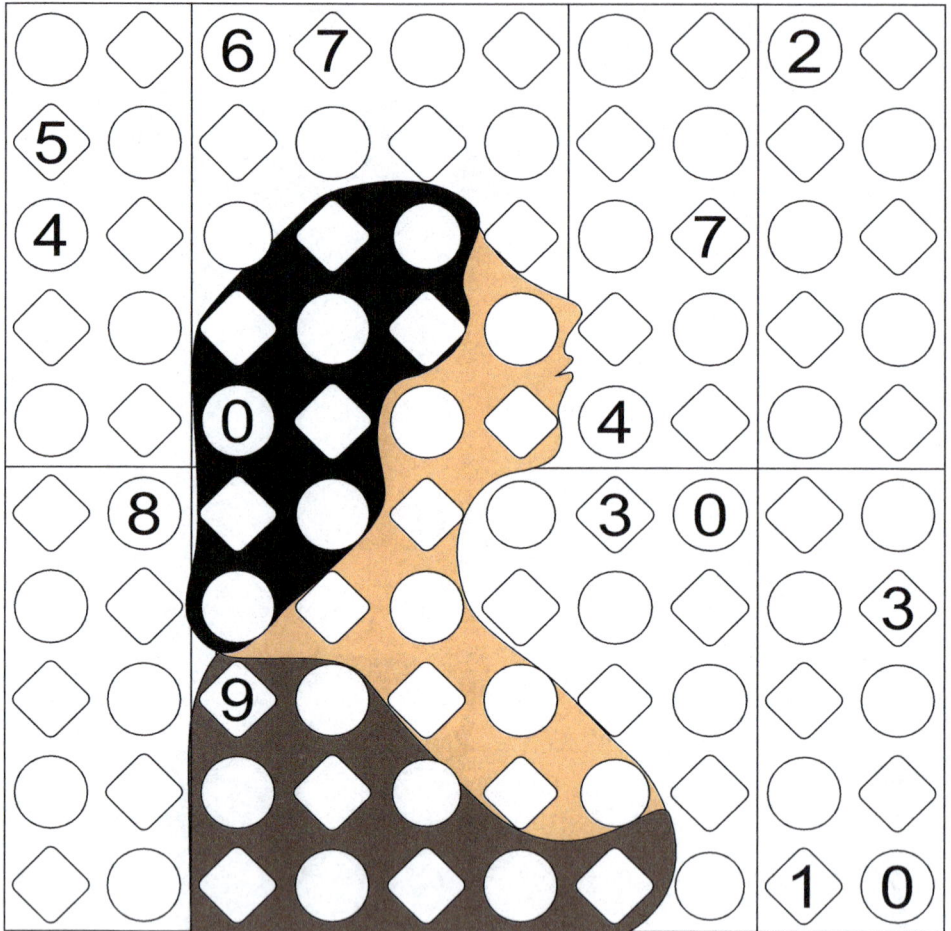

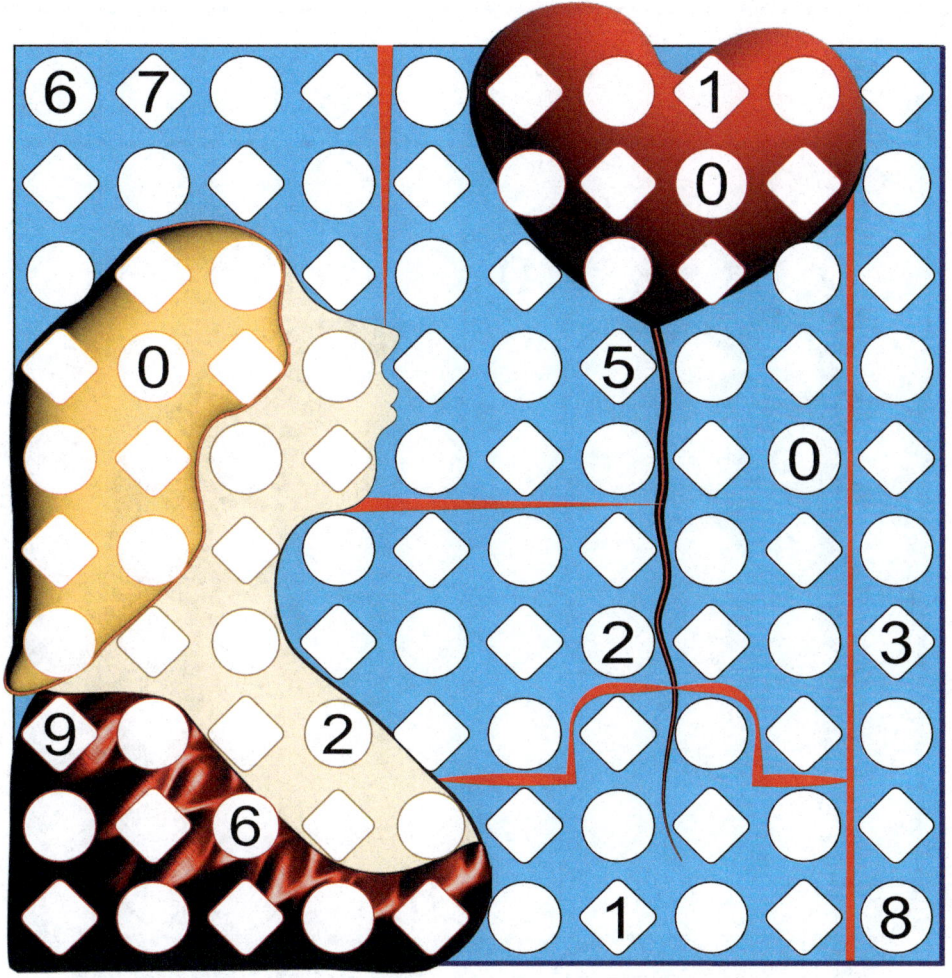

9

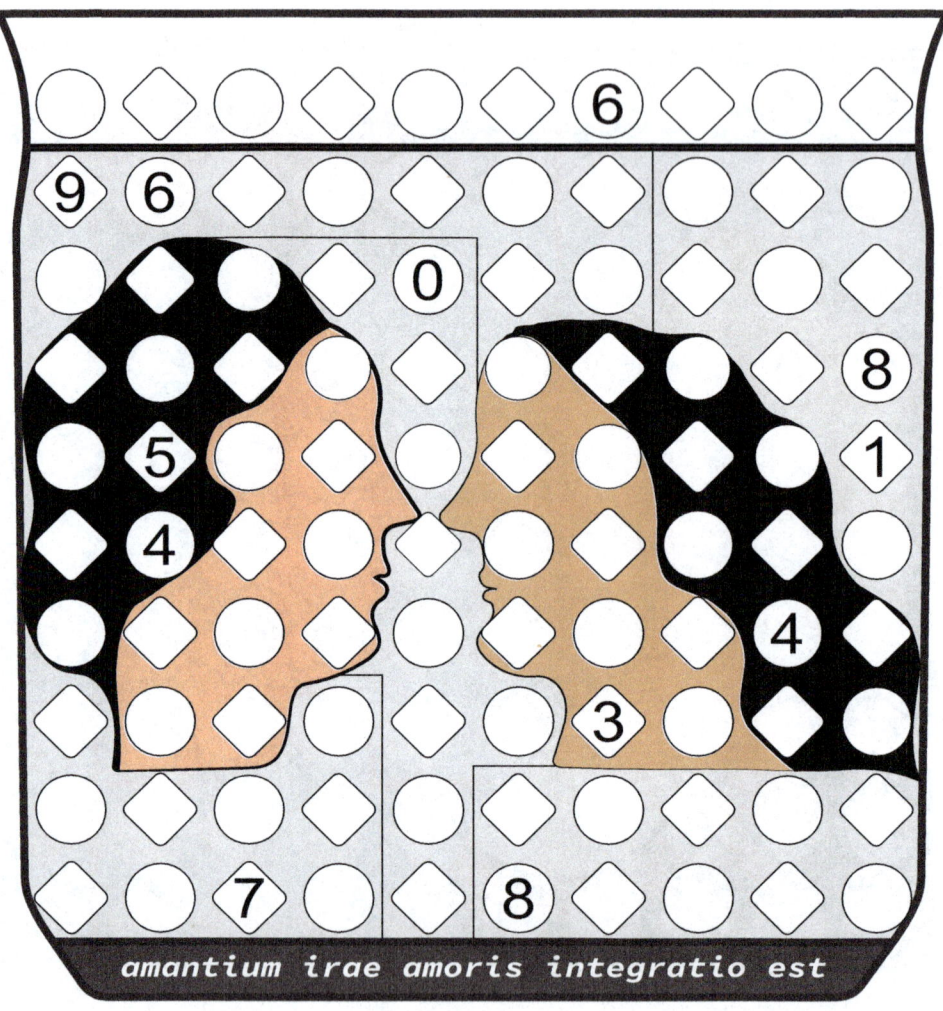

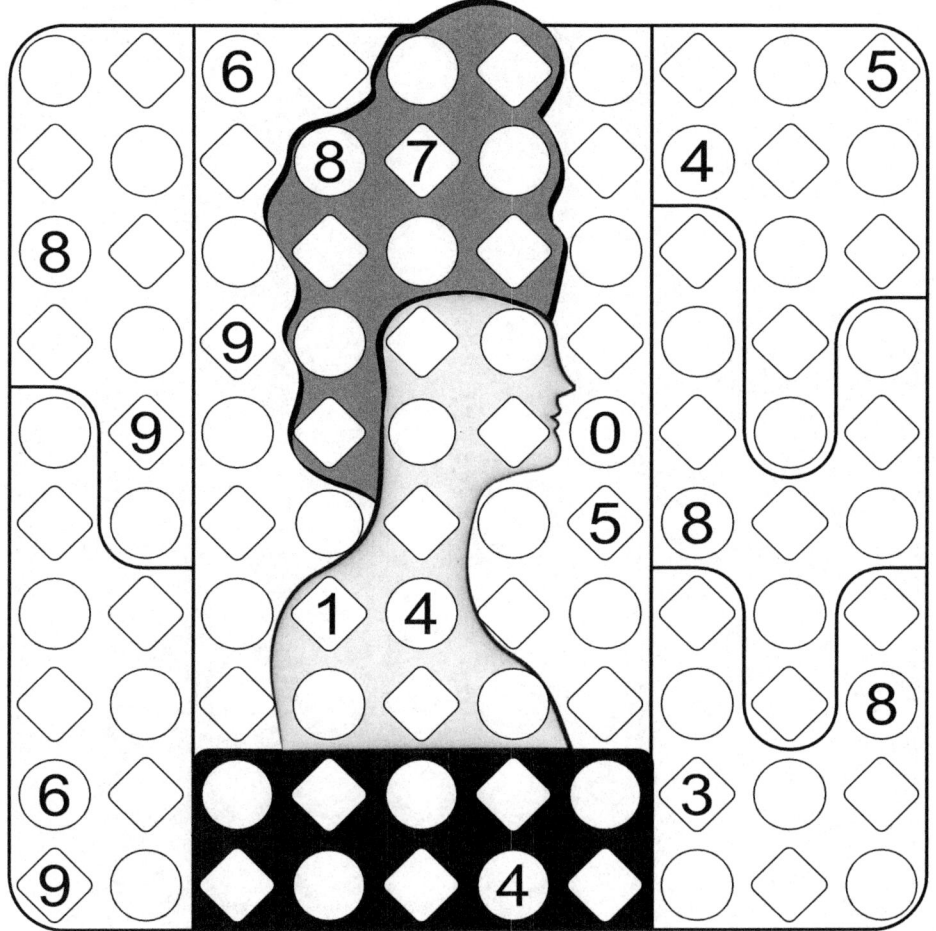

**Opal And Ruby Jewlery**

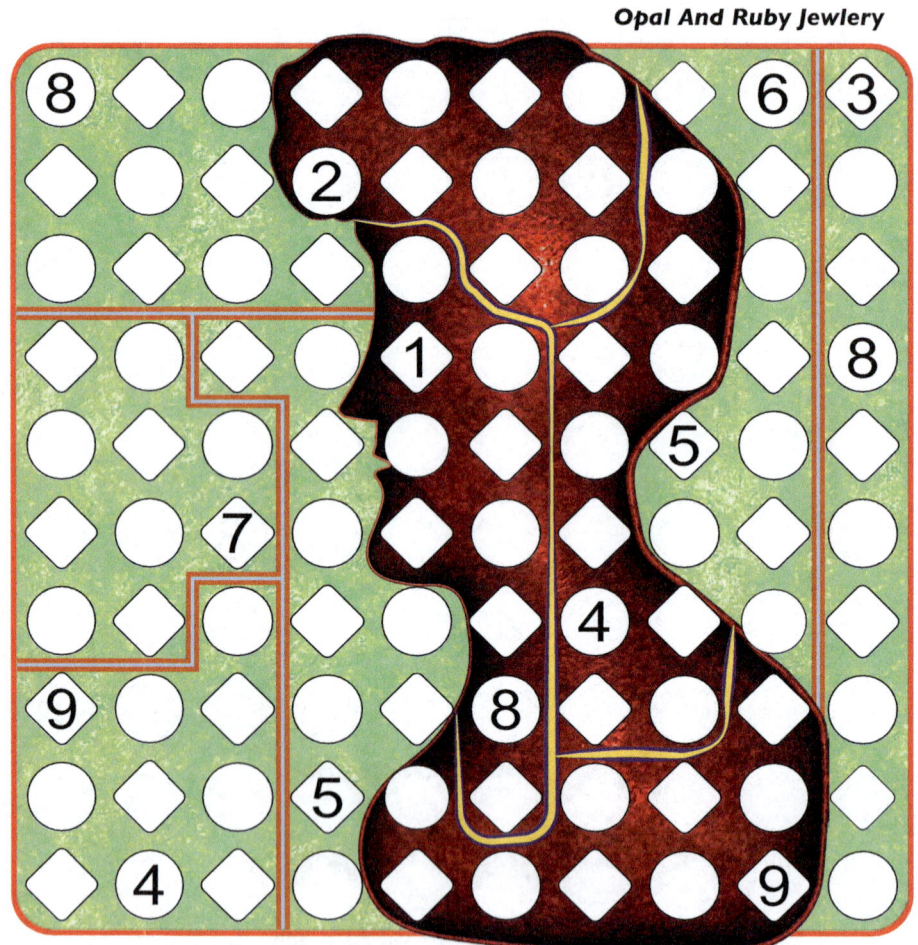

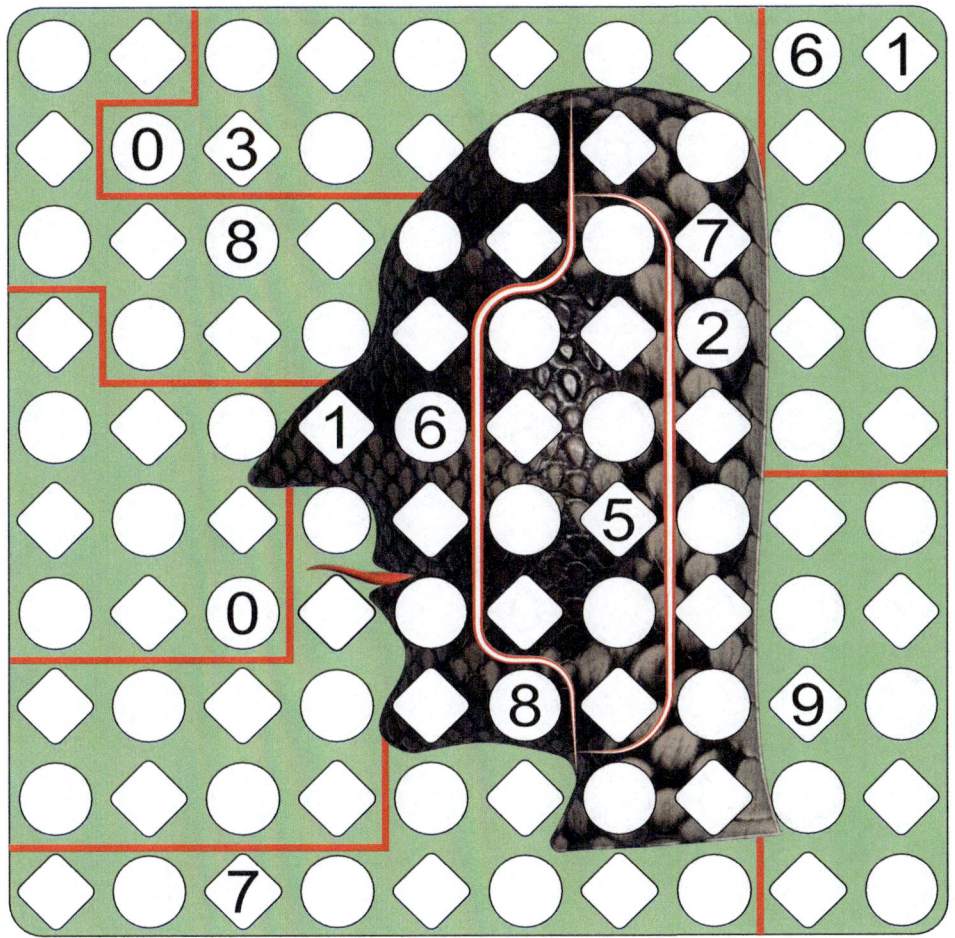

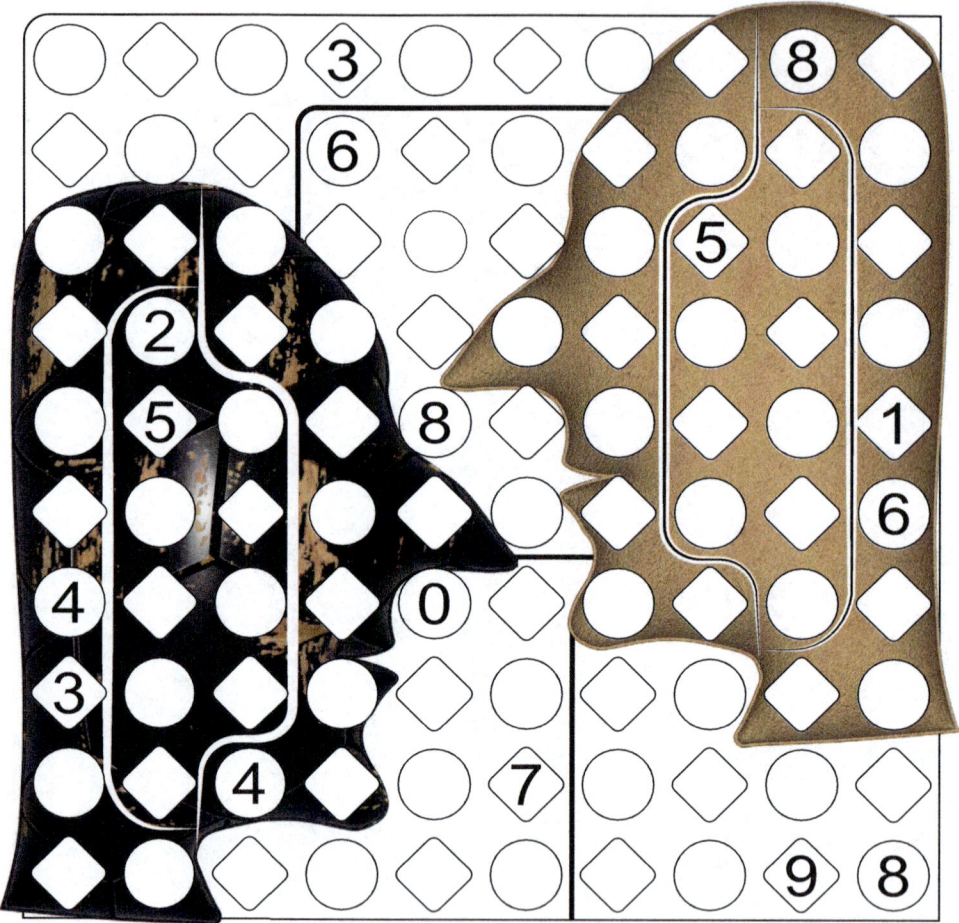

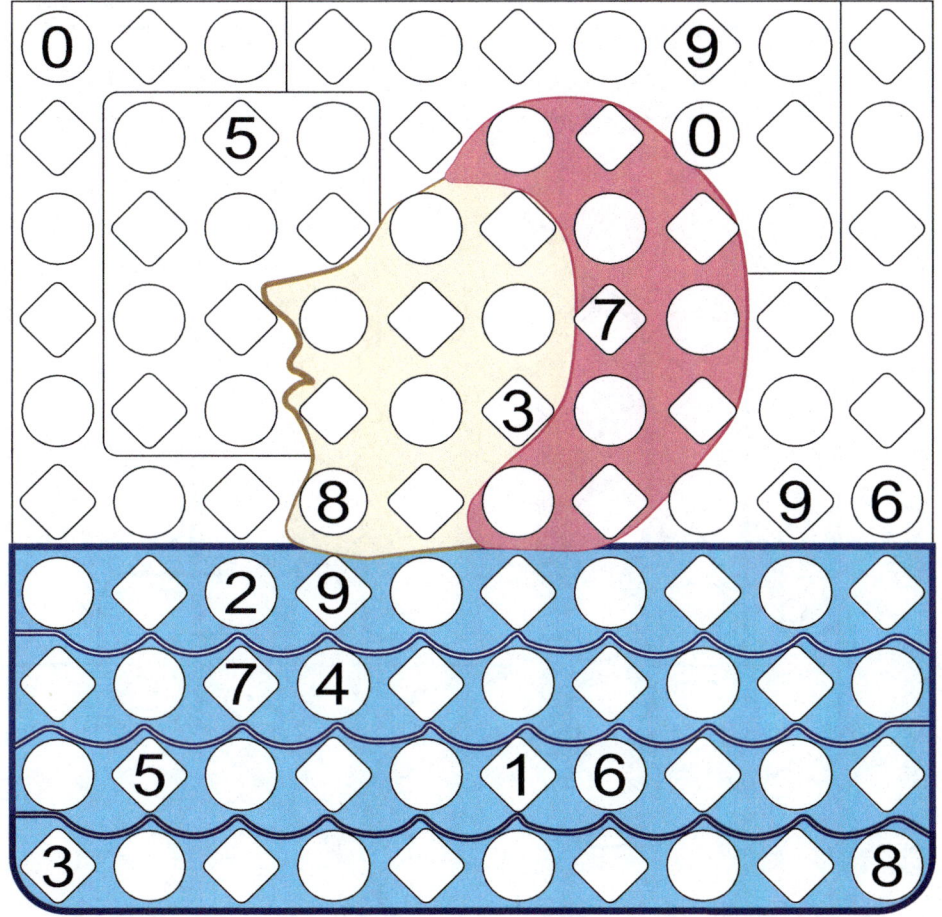

# Archaeological Finds

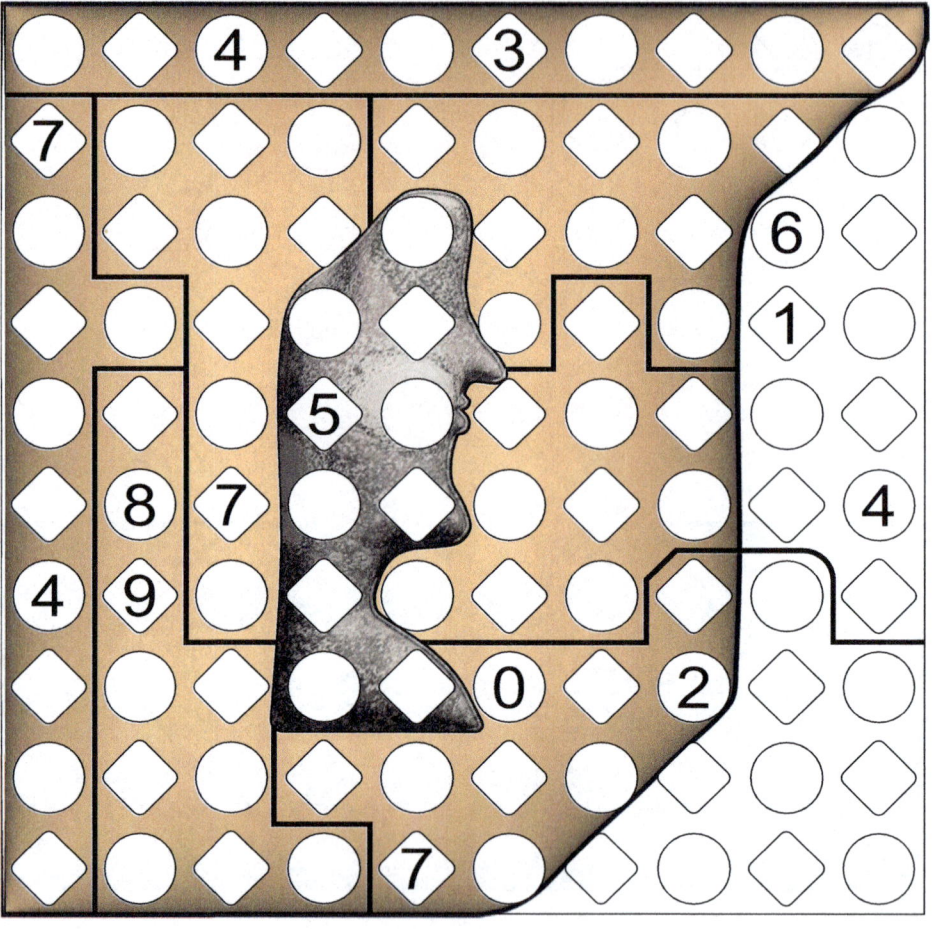

16

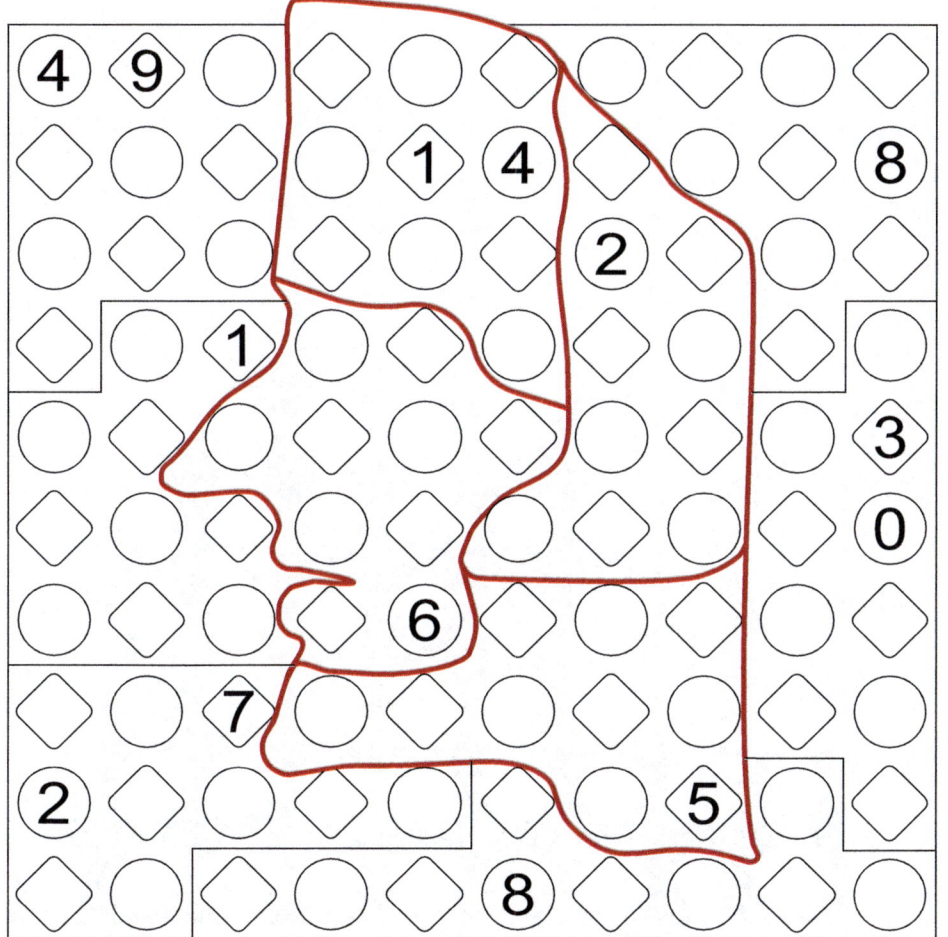

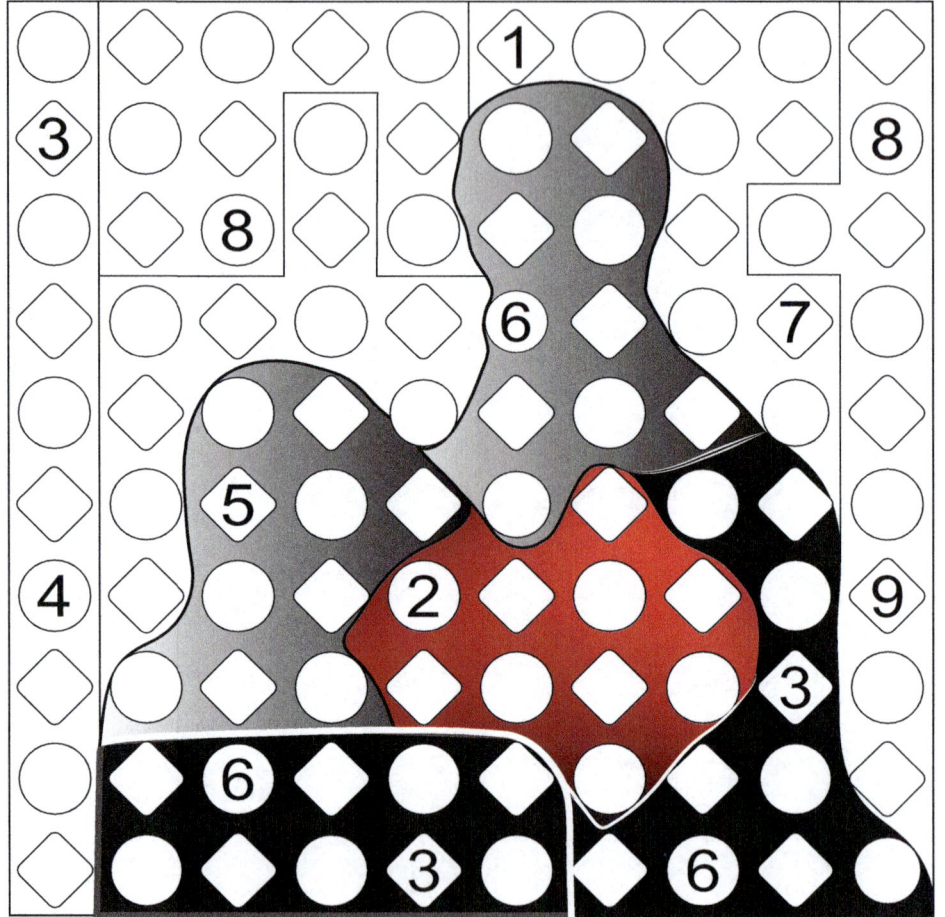

## The First Time

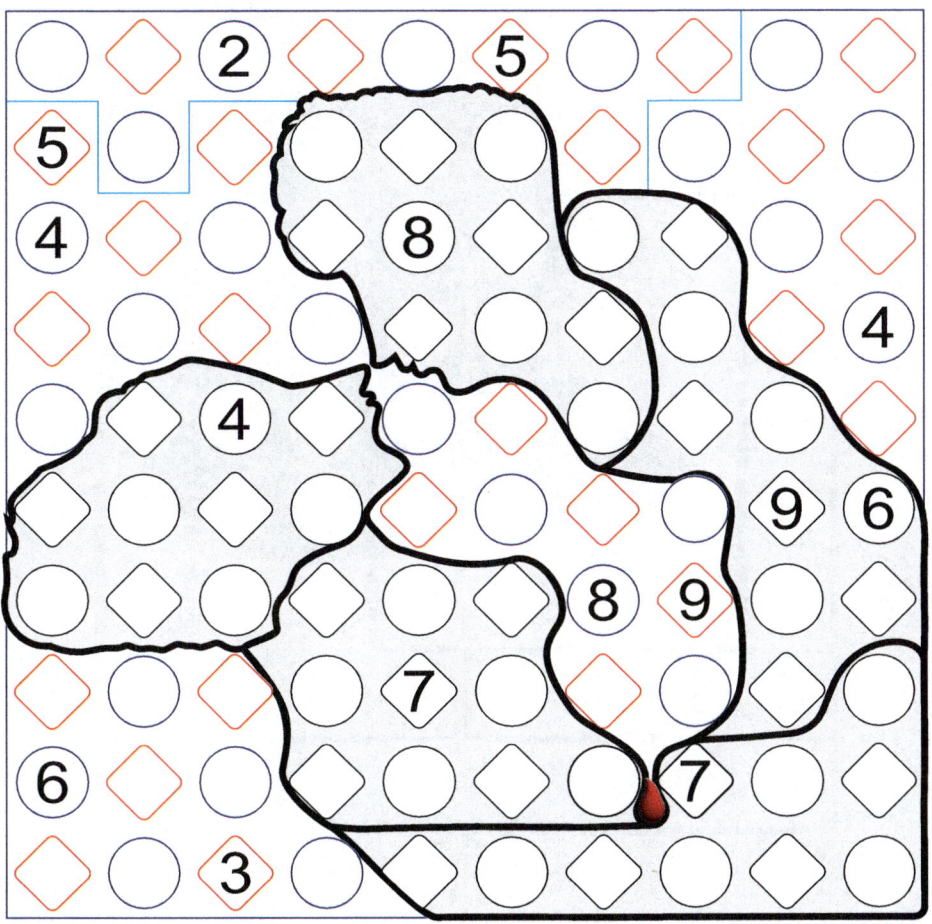

19

## Queen of Spades

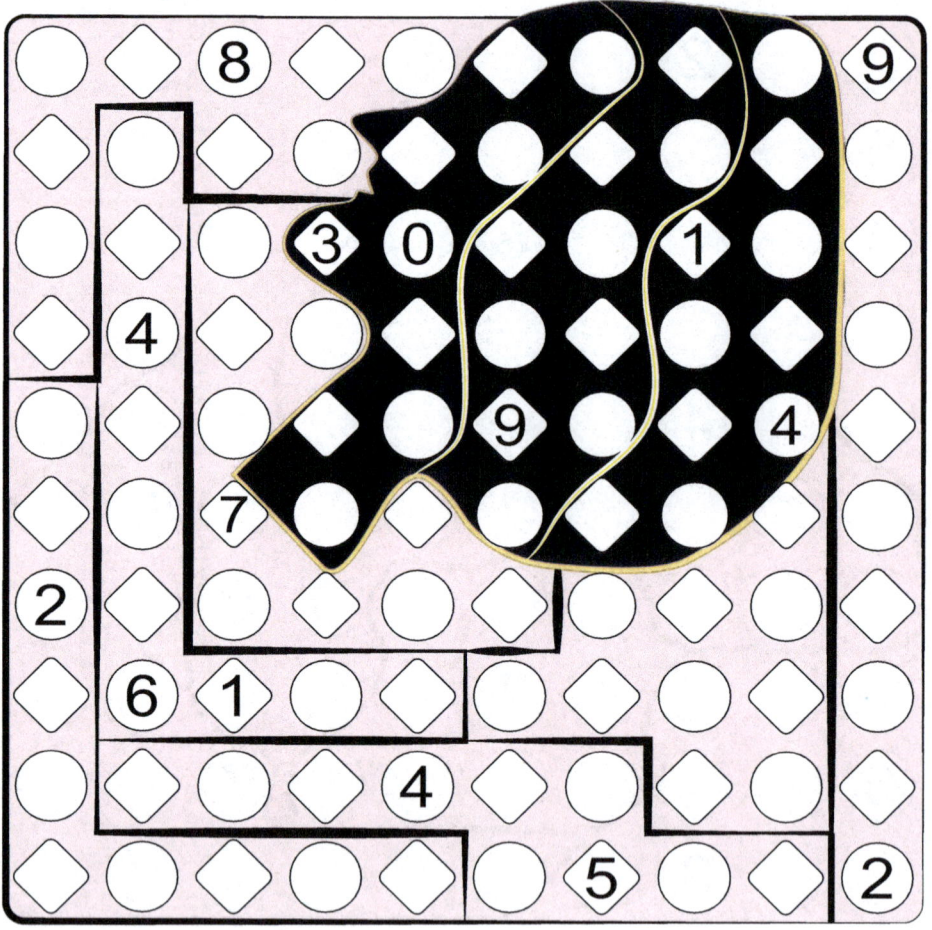

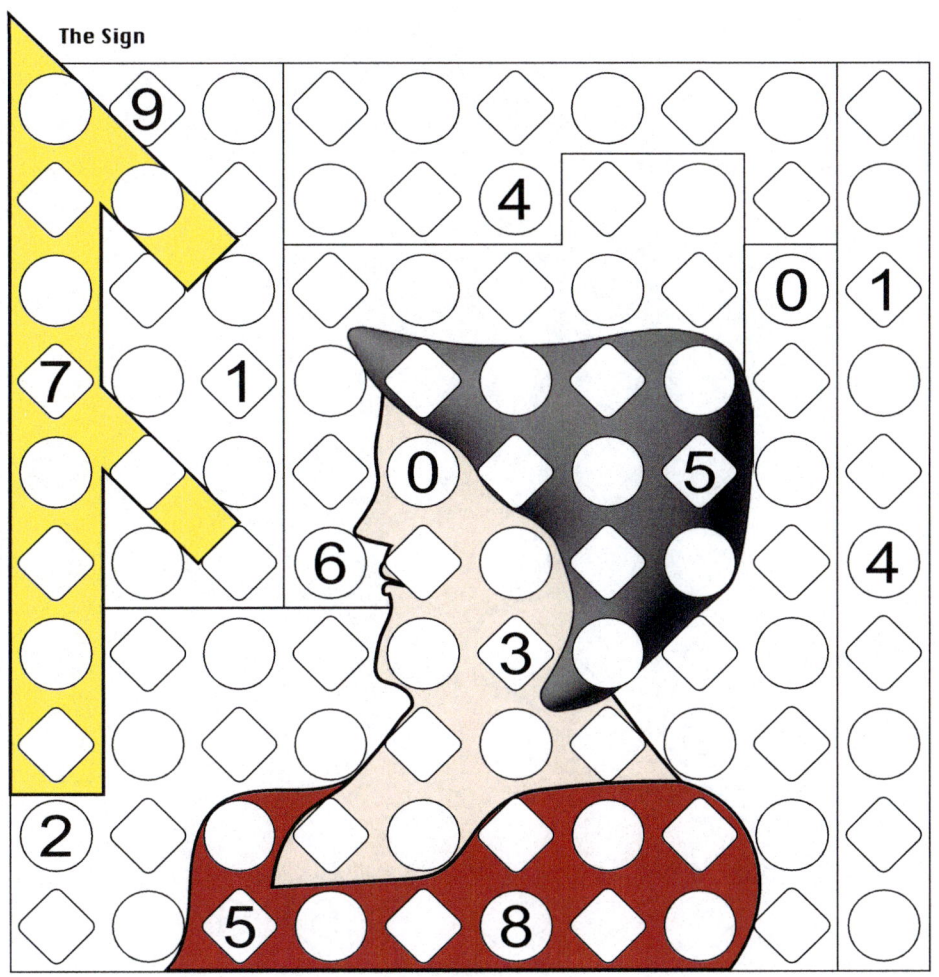

The Sign

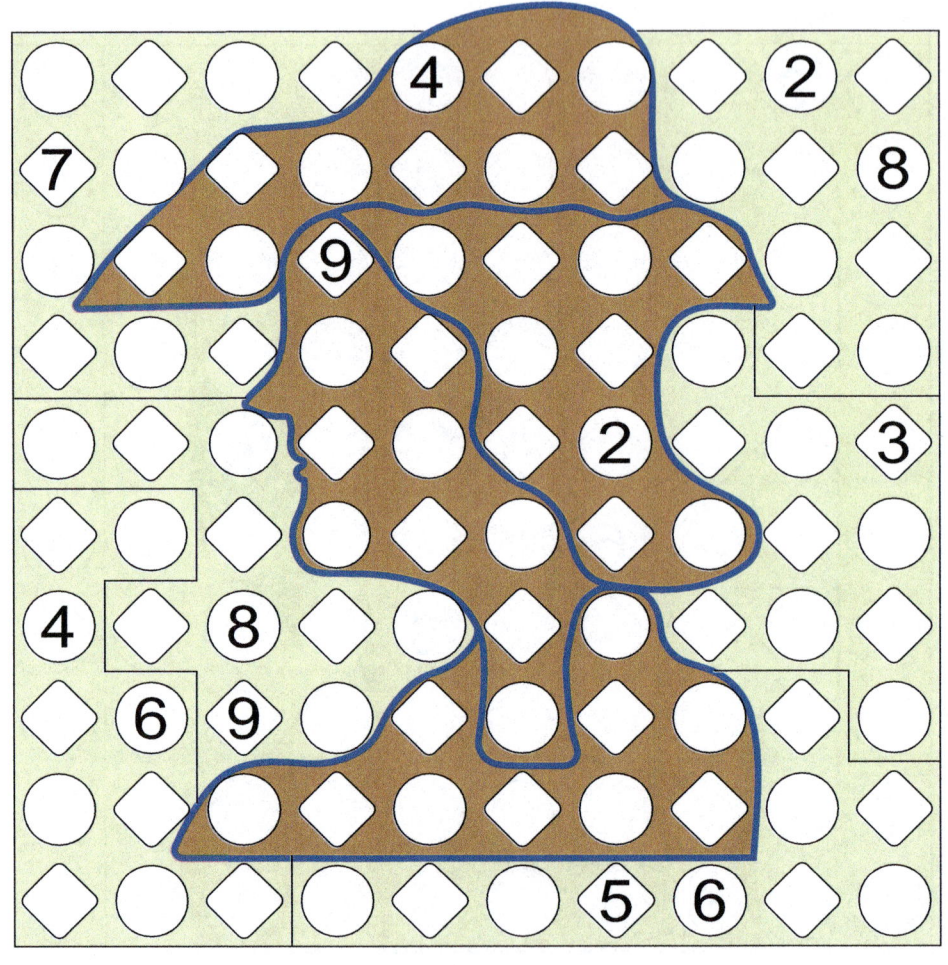

**Astral Projection & the Dreaming Body**

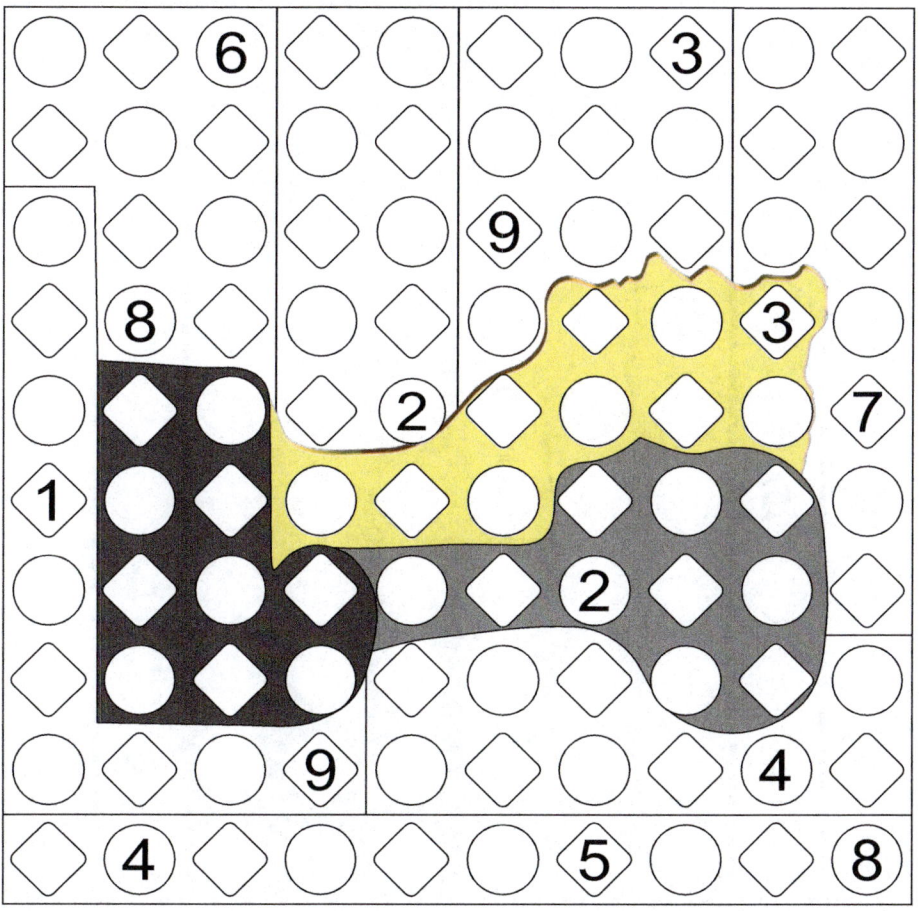

23

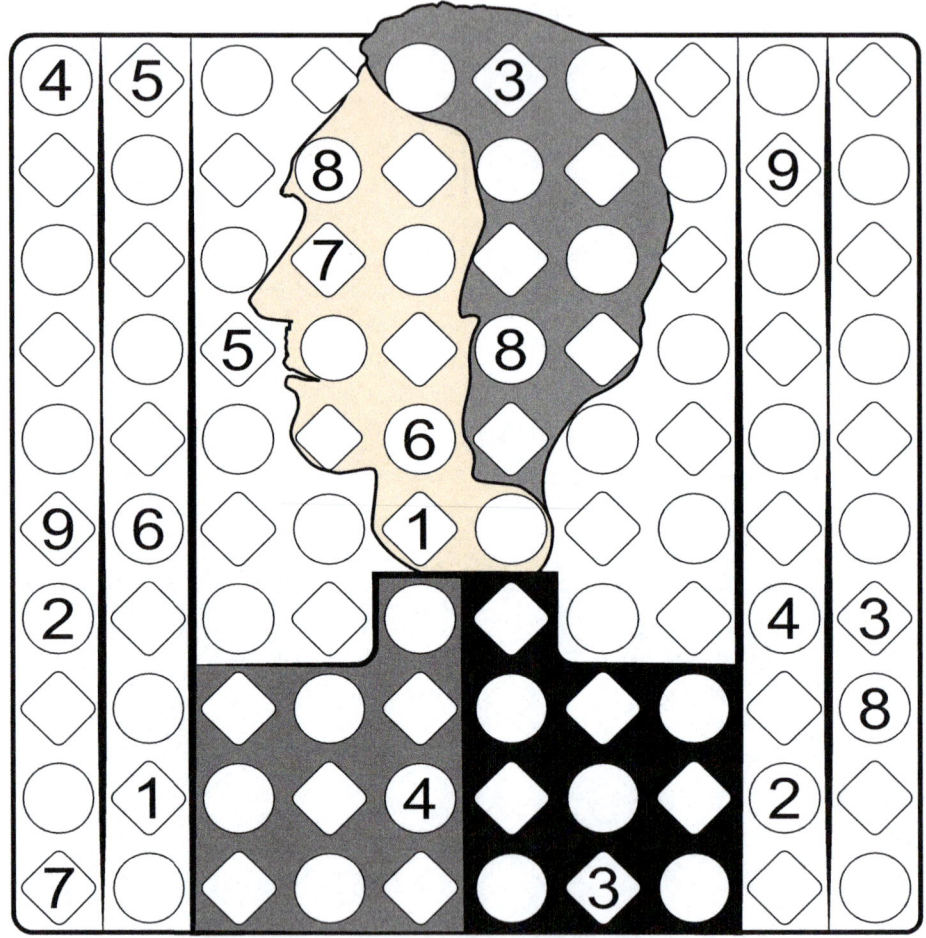

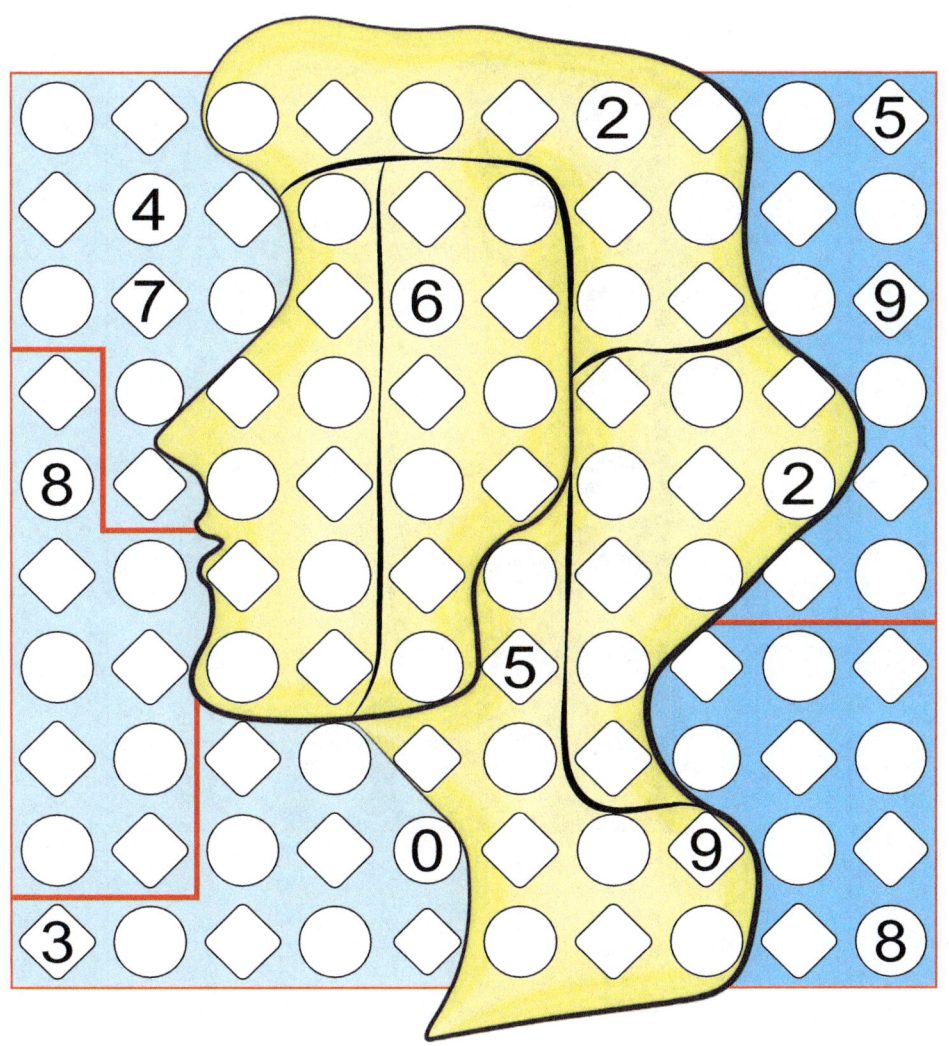

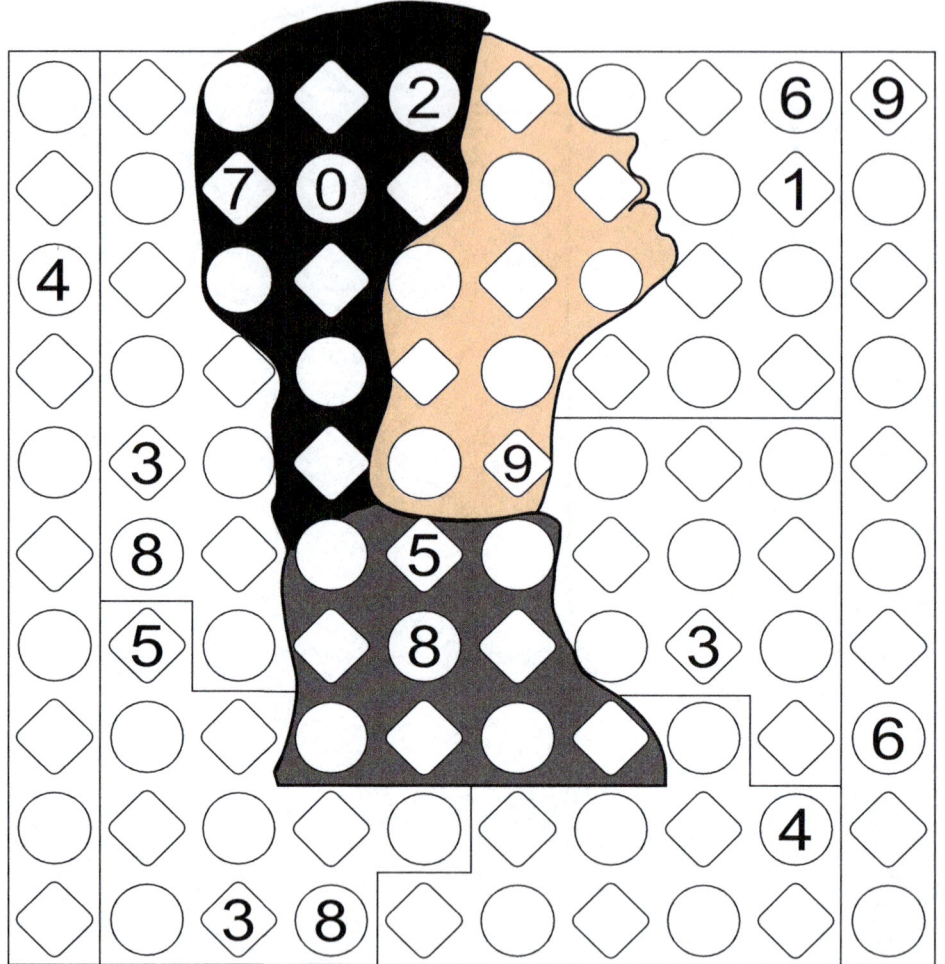

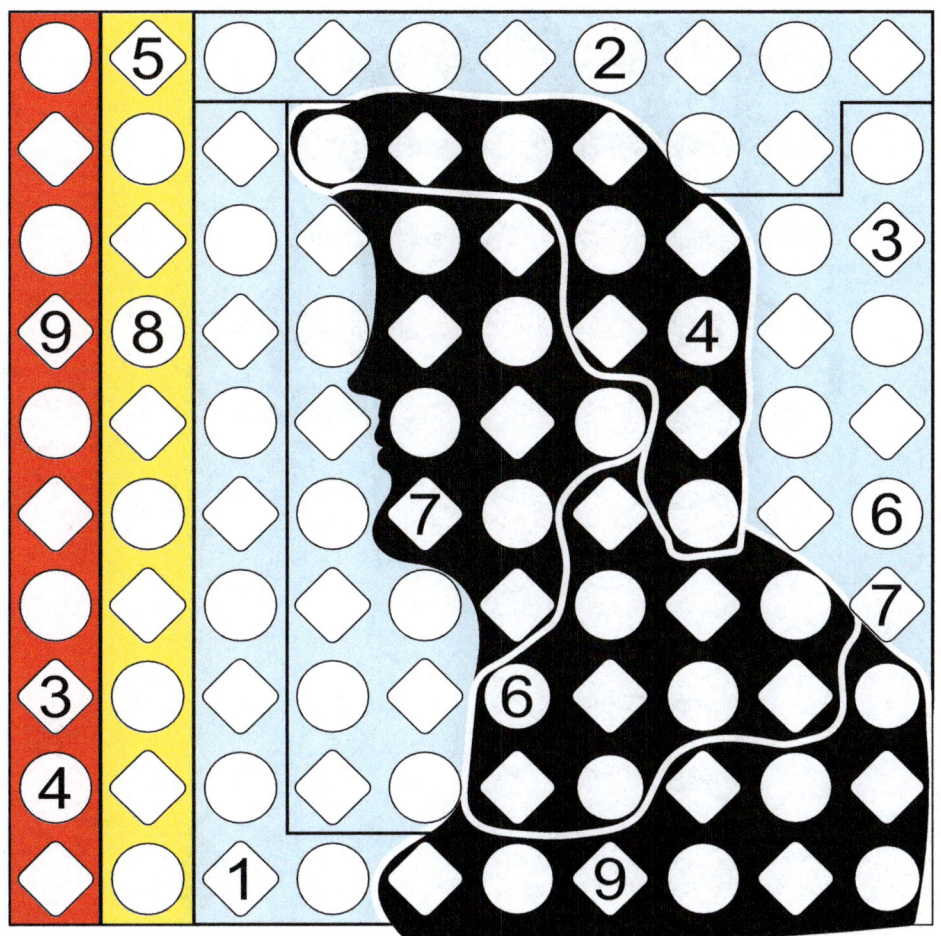

27

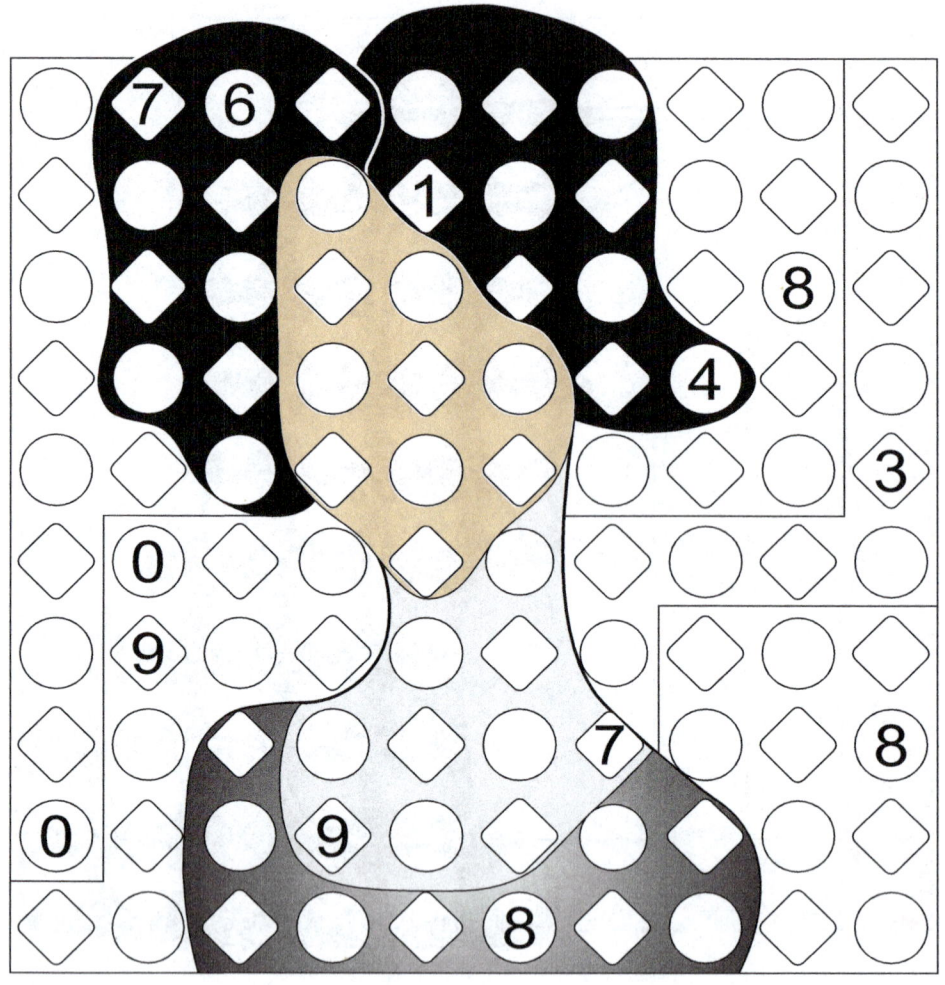

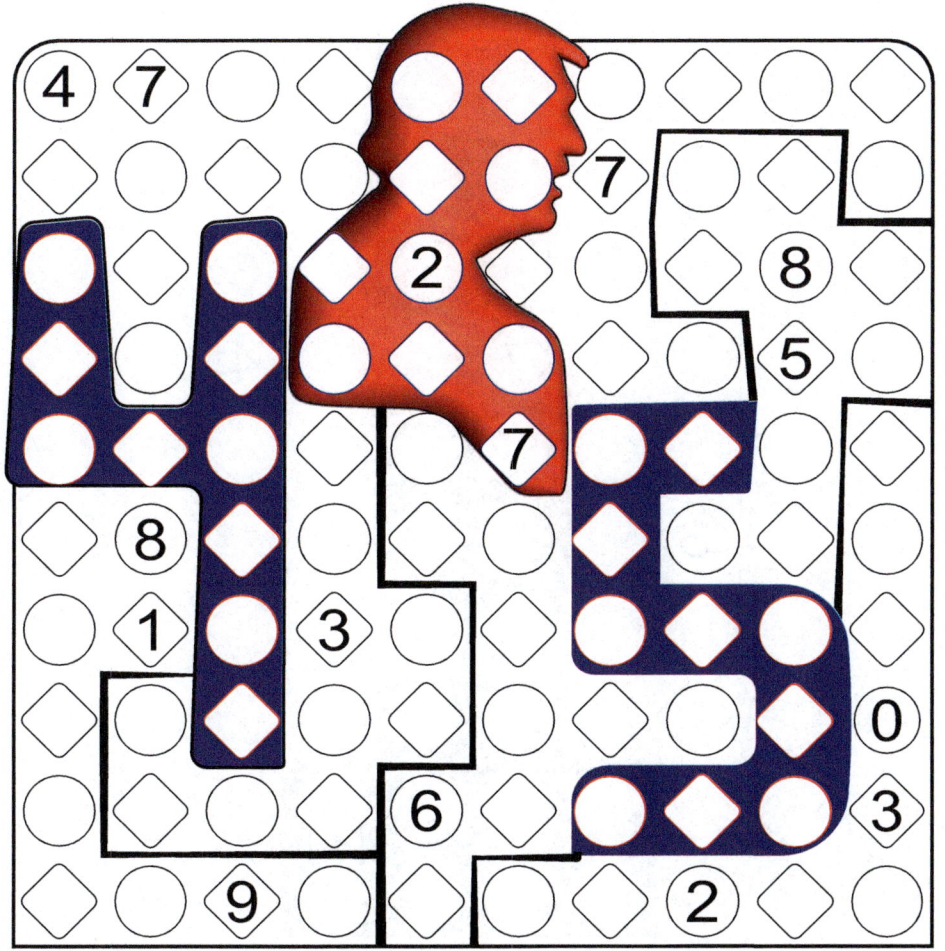

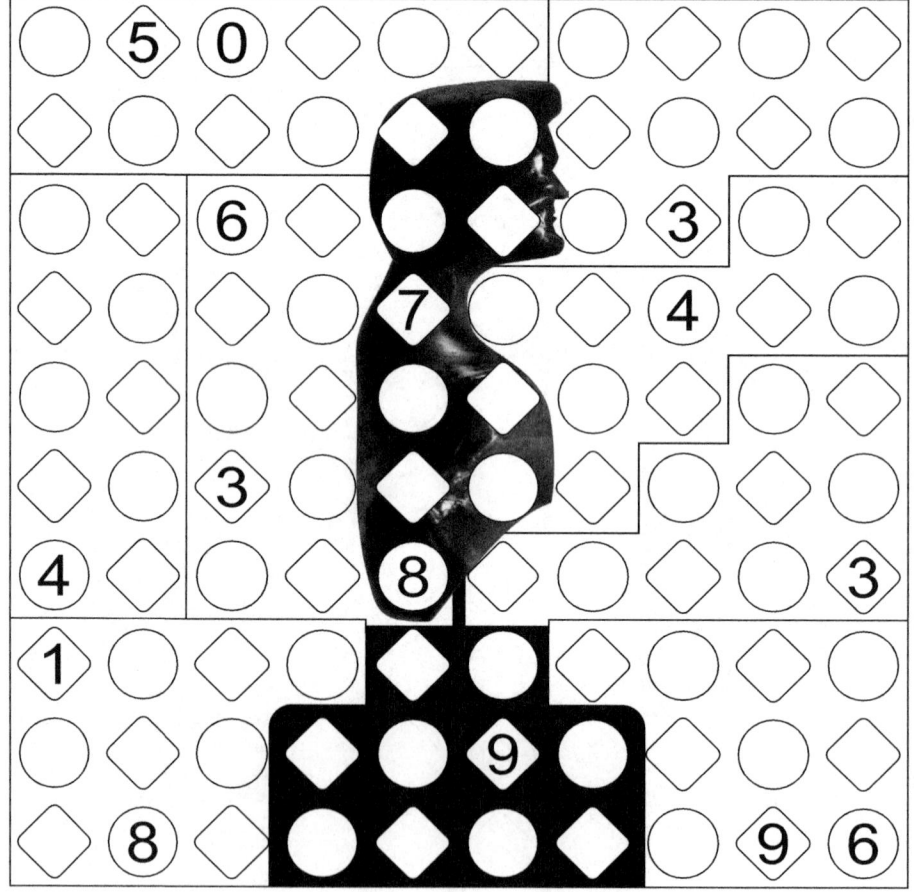

# The View From Above

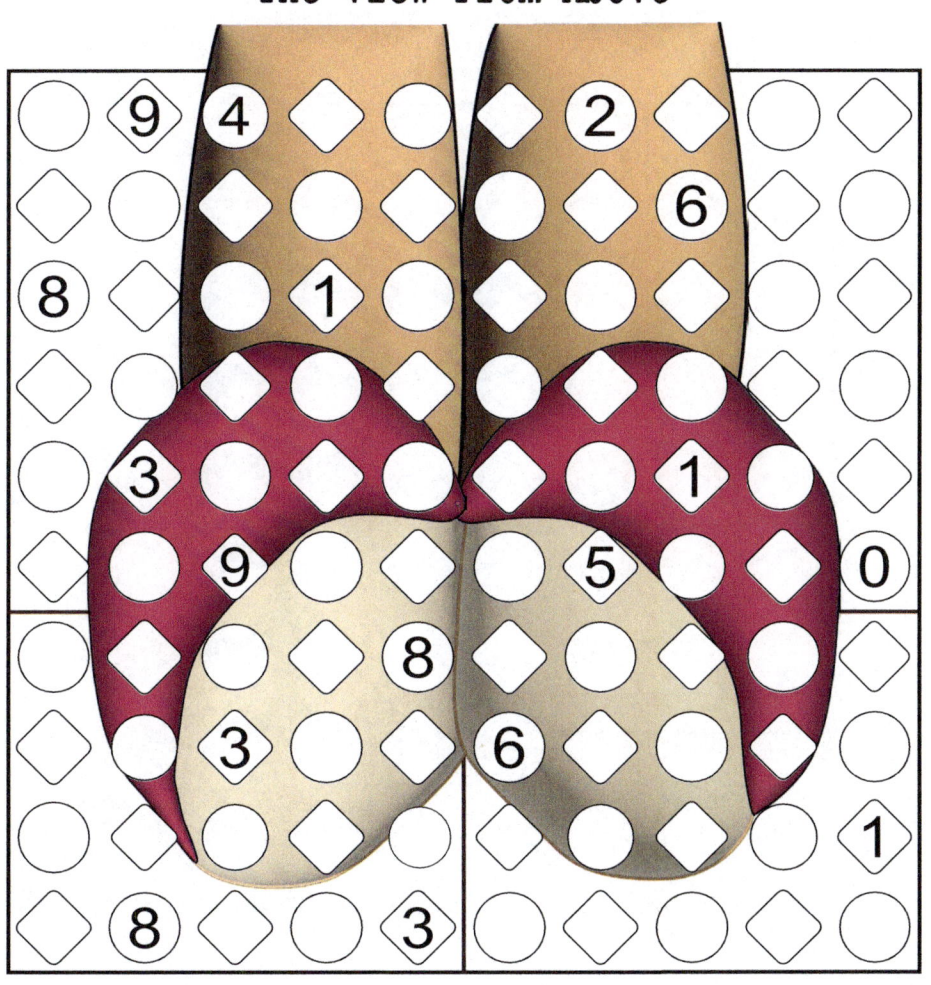

## In Gossip Mode

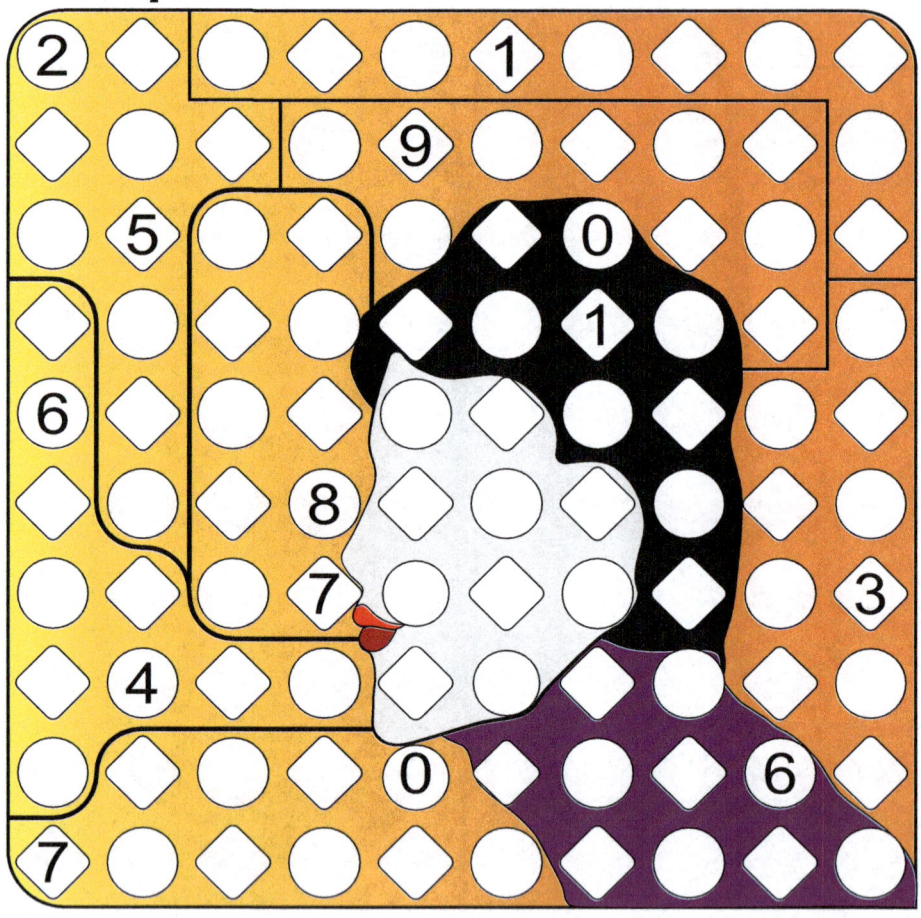

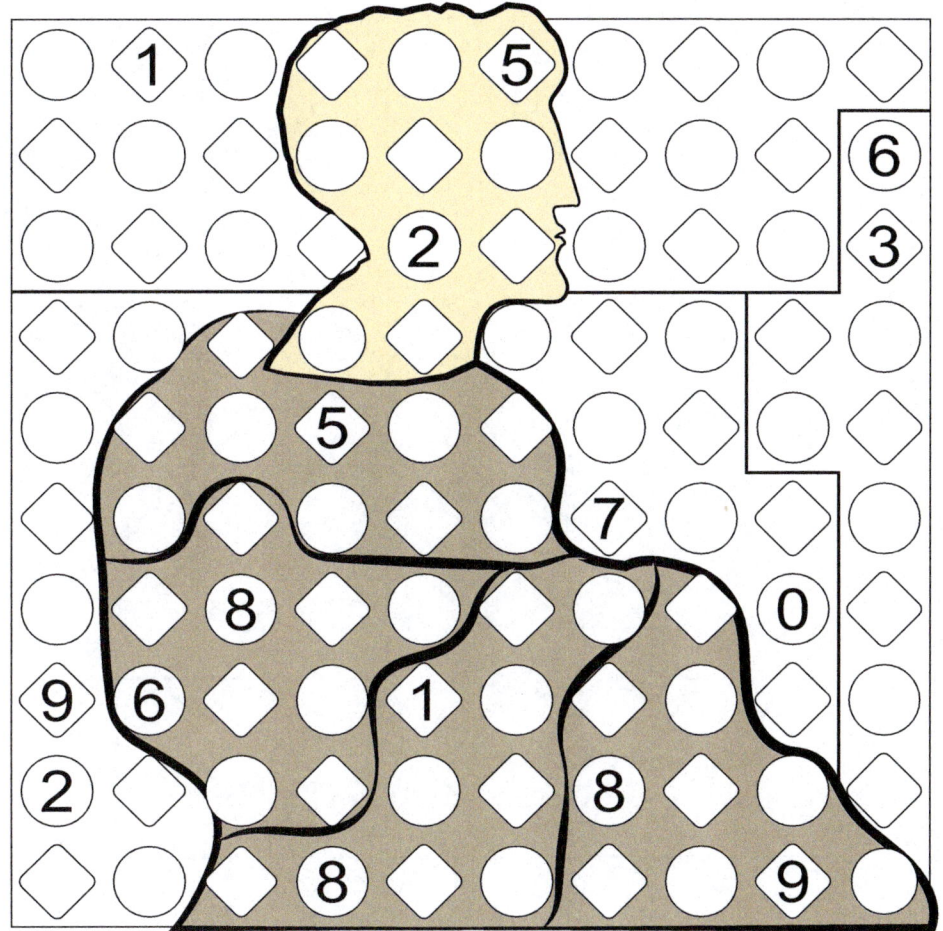

**The Real Question**

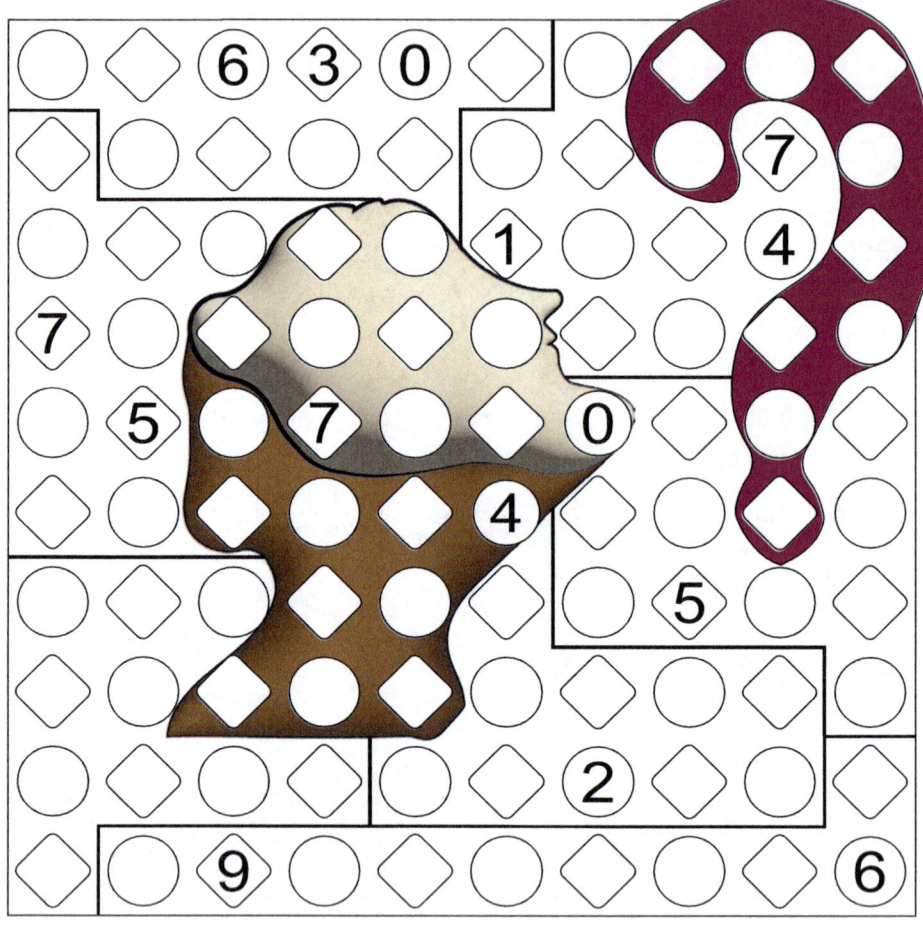

34

# Synergy

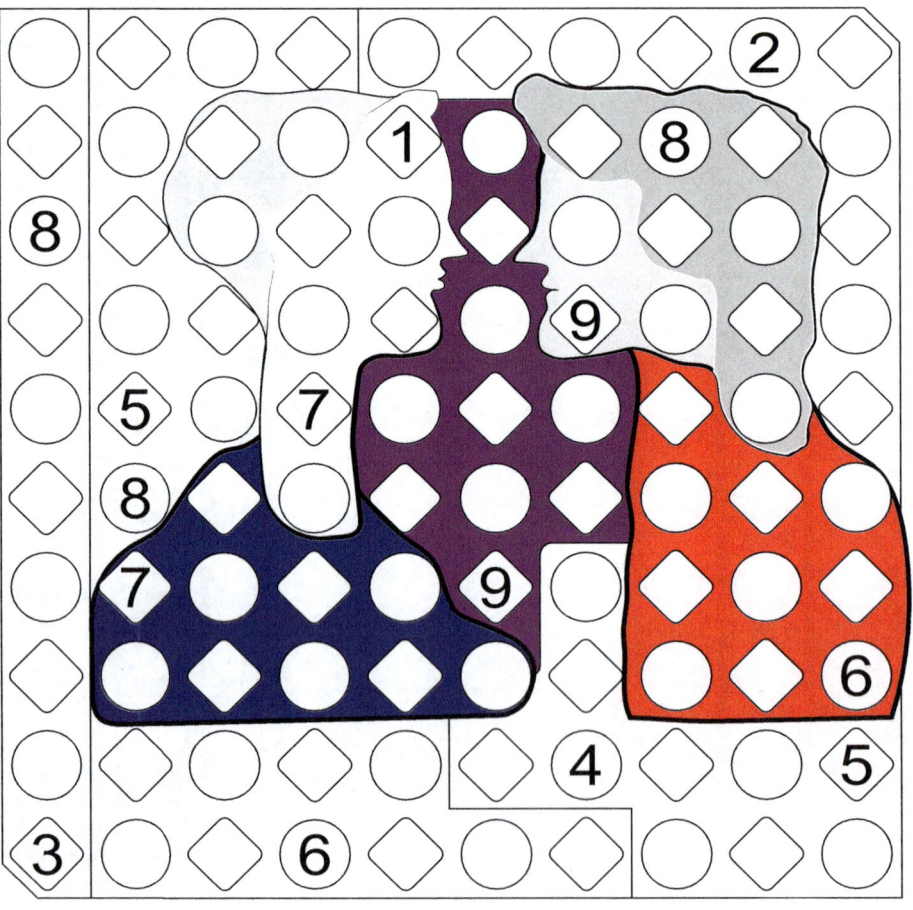

## The Arguments

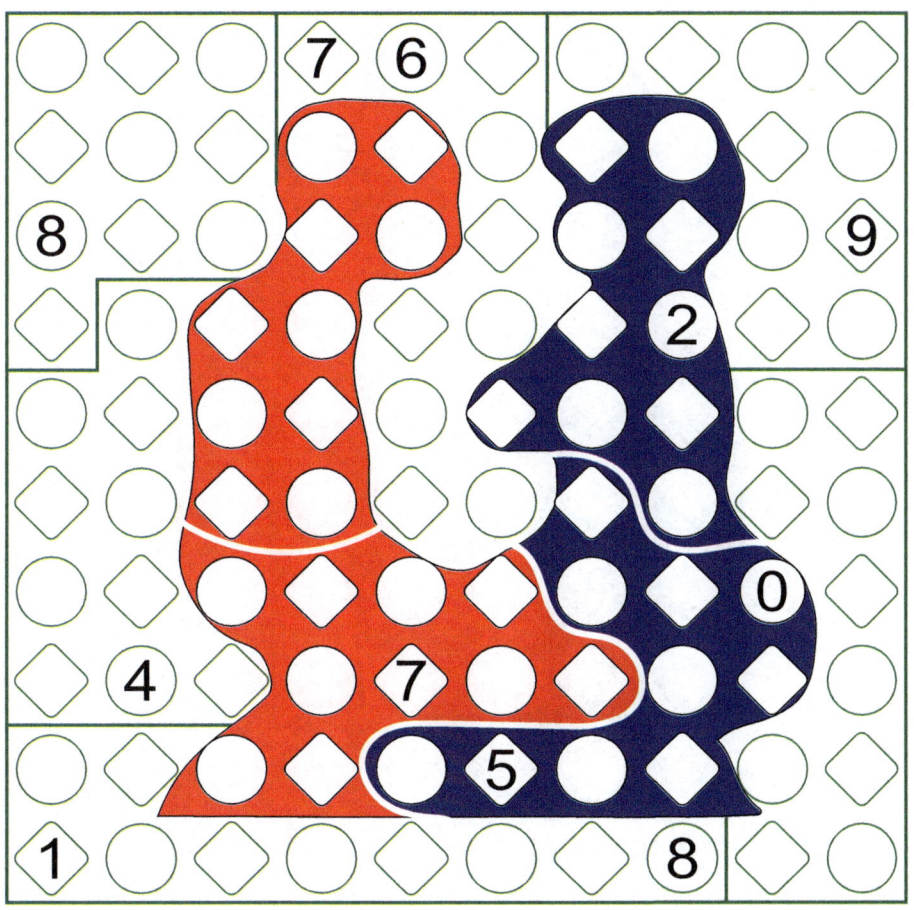

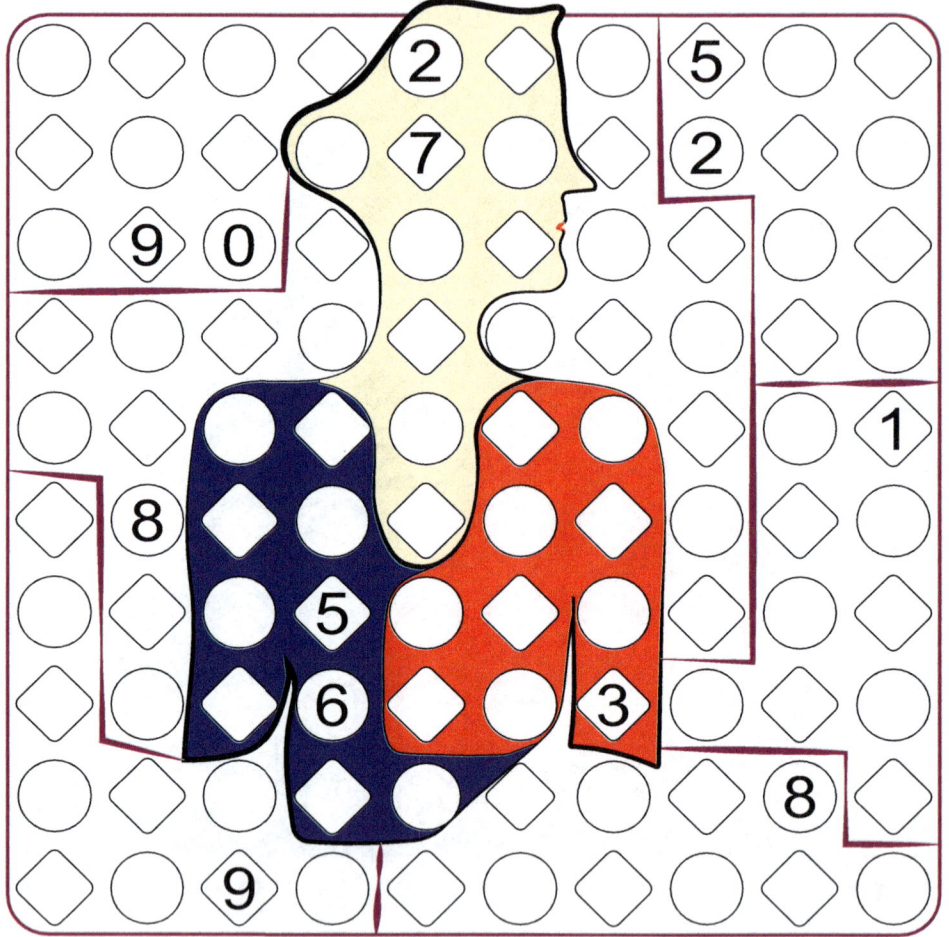

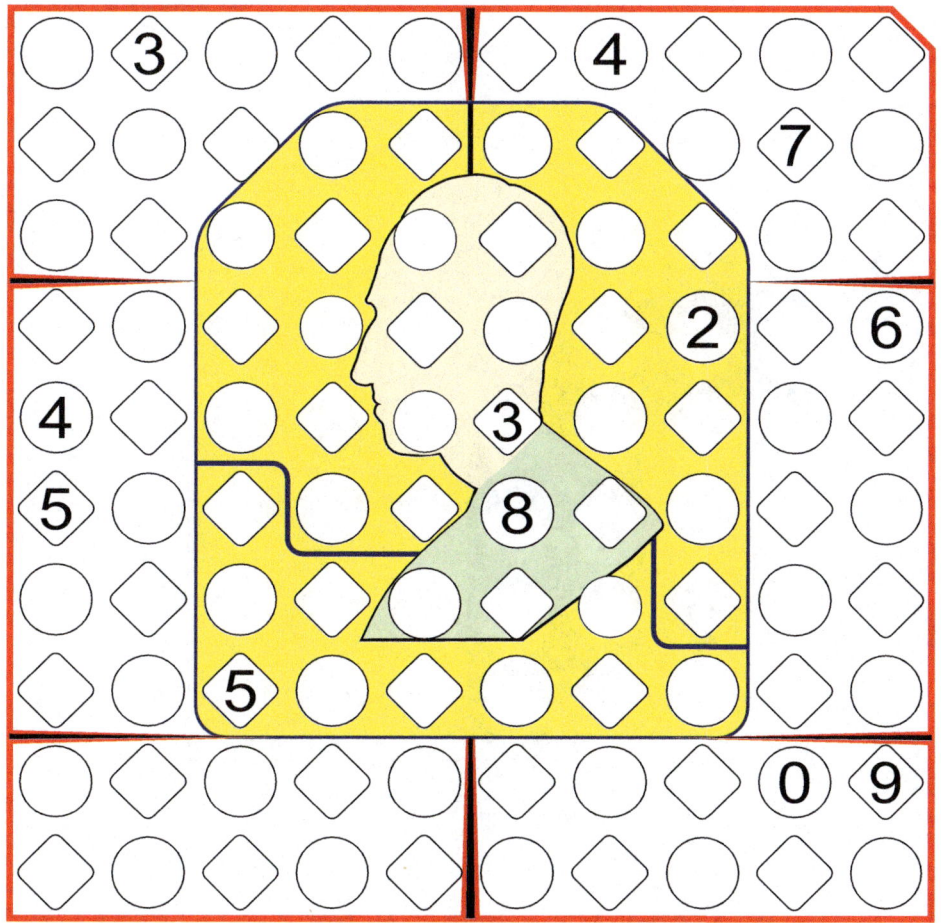

### The Man with the Halo

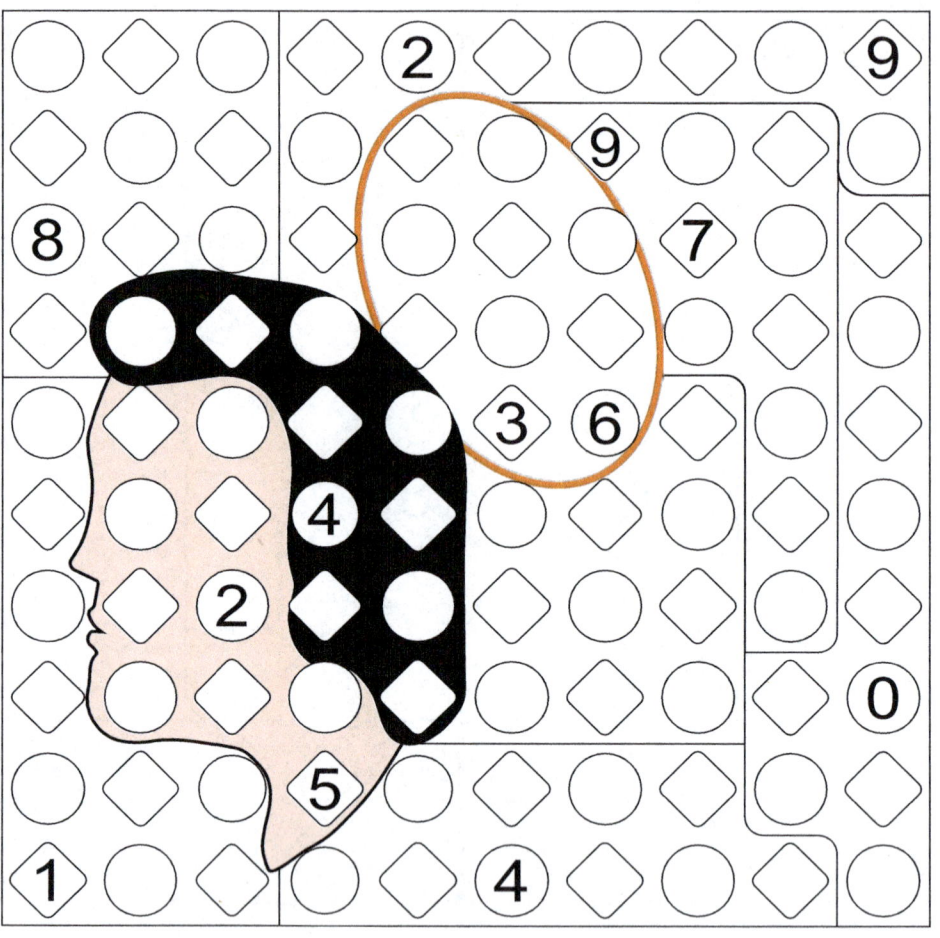

40

## Staring Into the Abyss

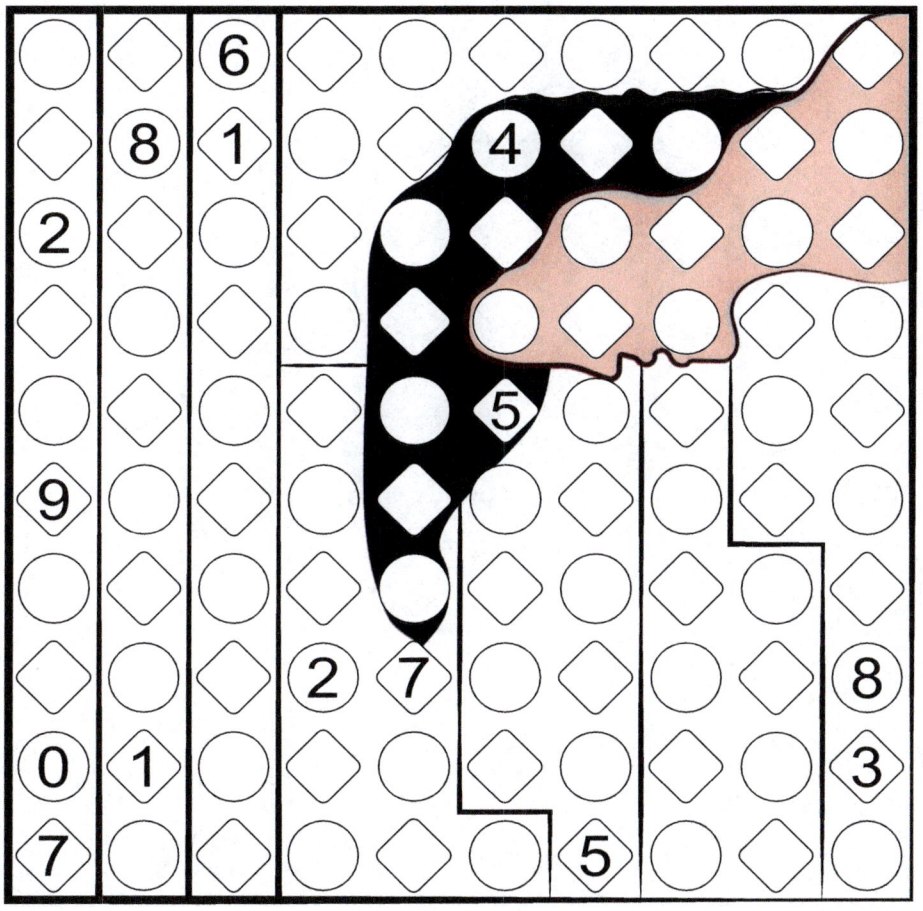

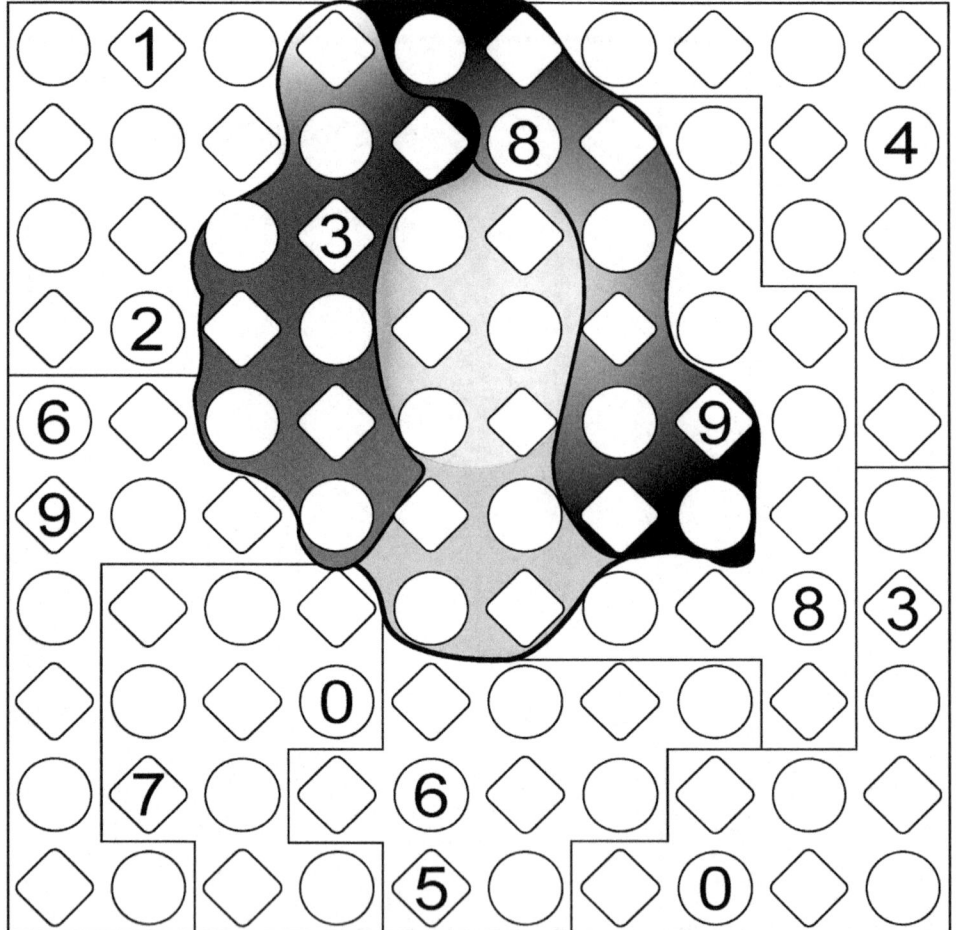

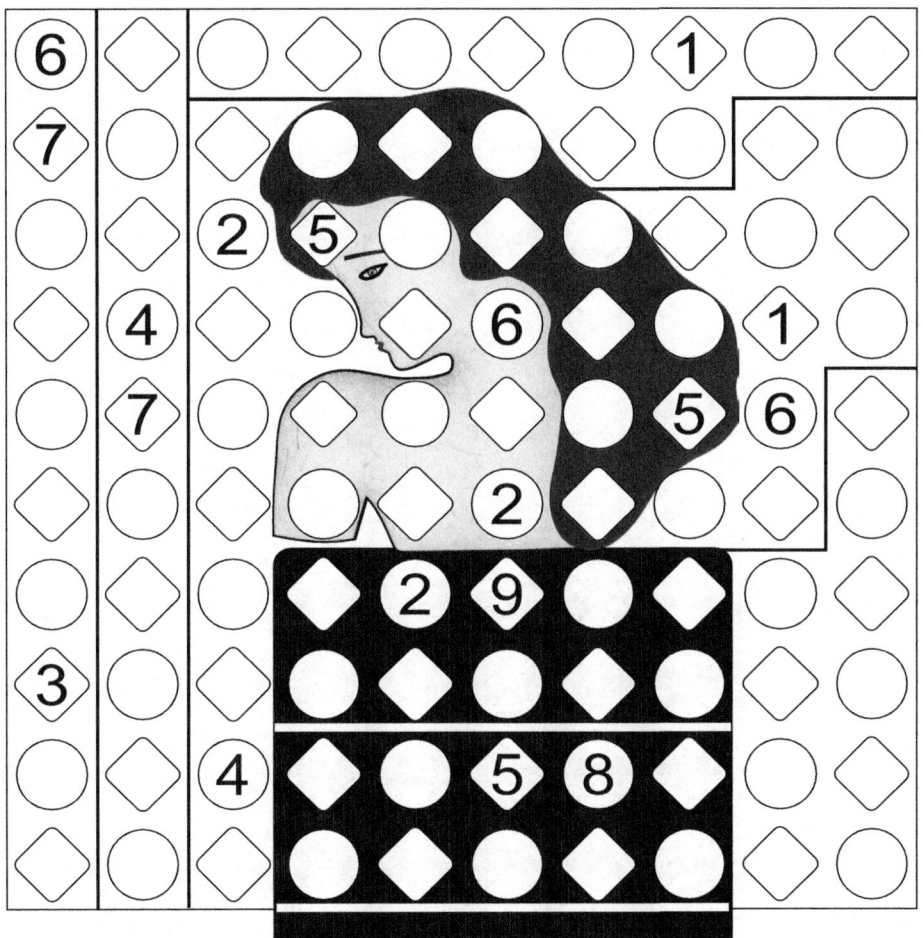

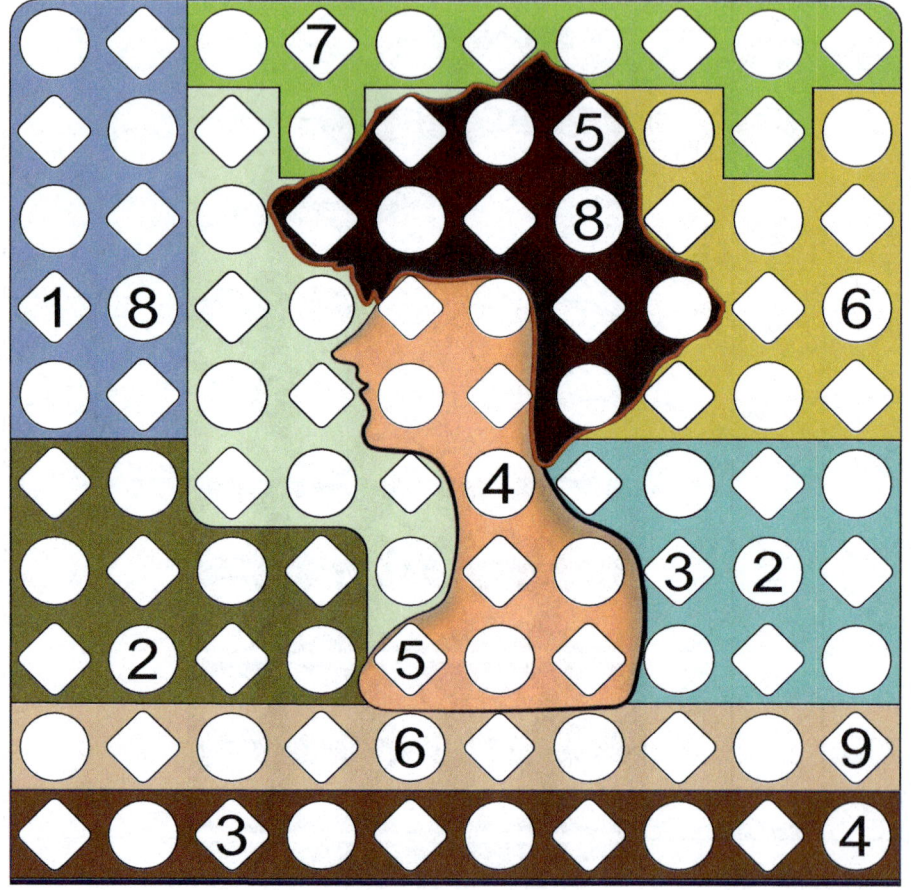

# A Man and a Woman

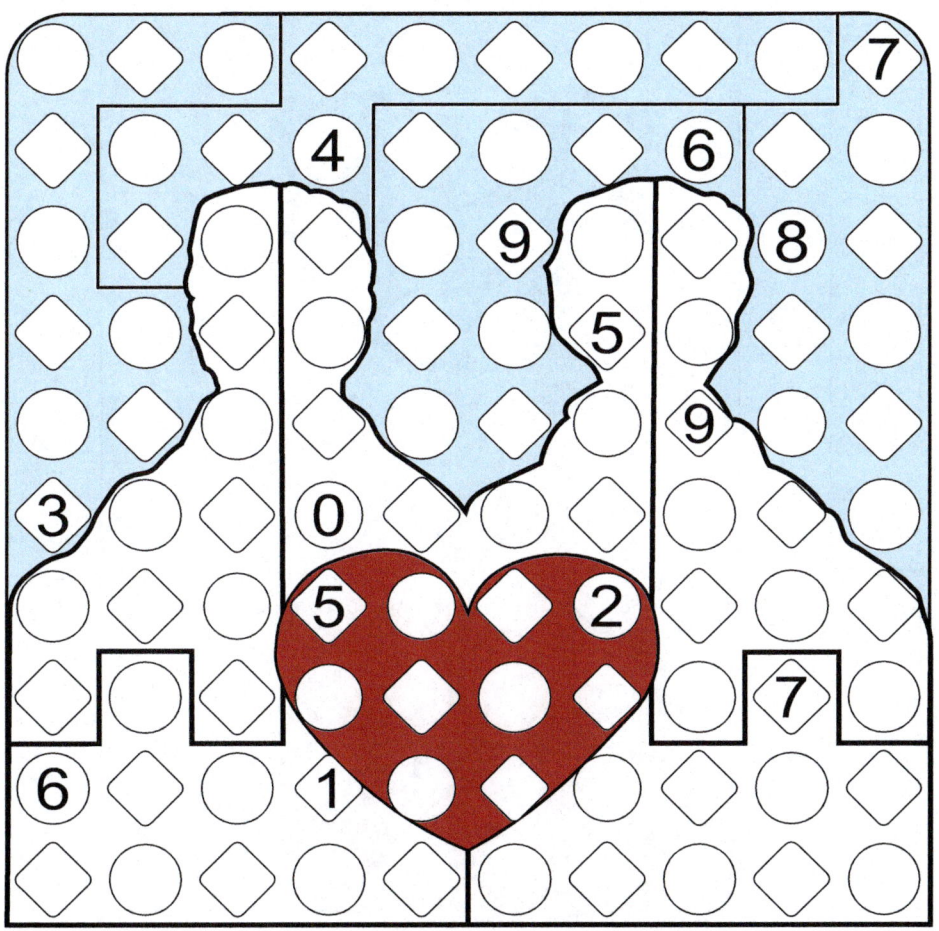

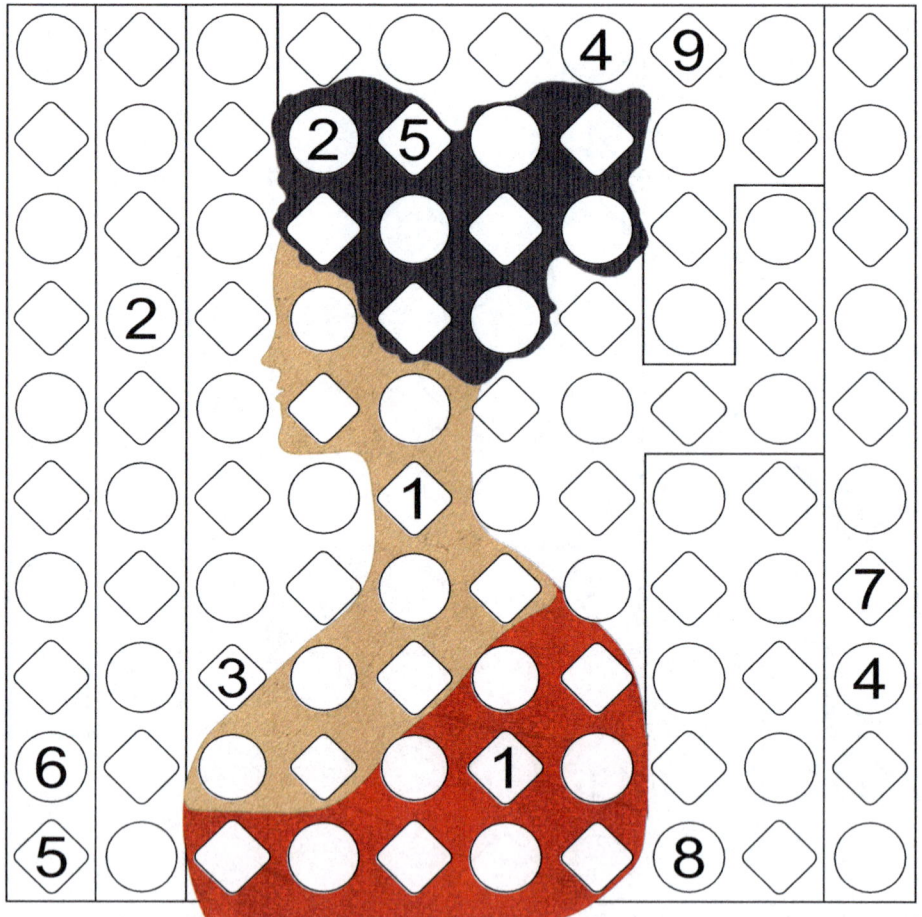

# The Scream

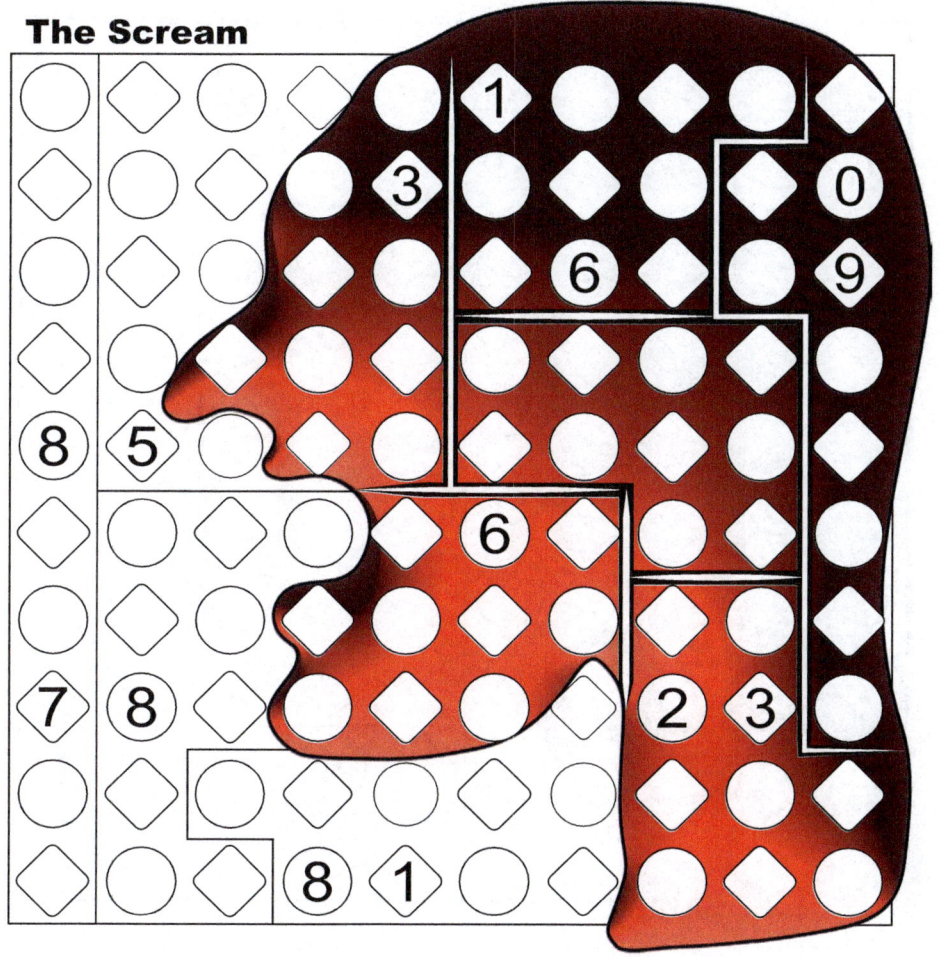

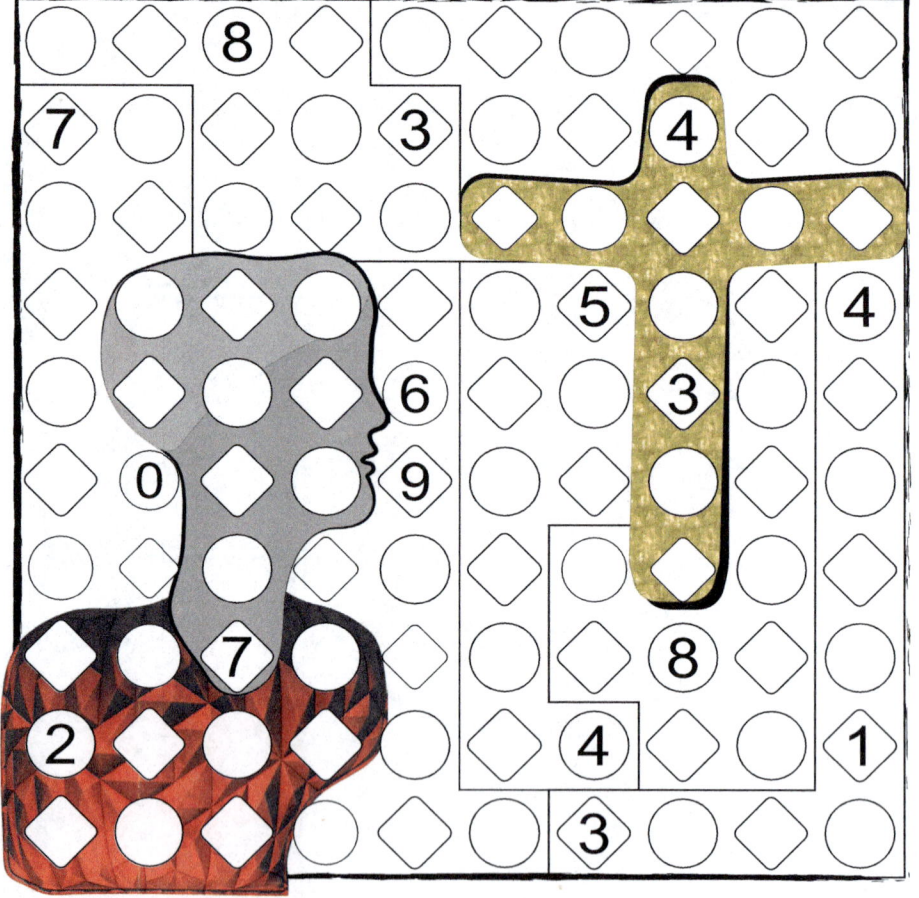

# The Sphinx

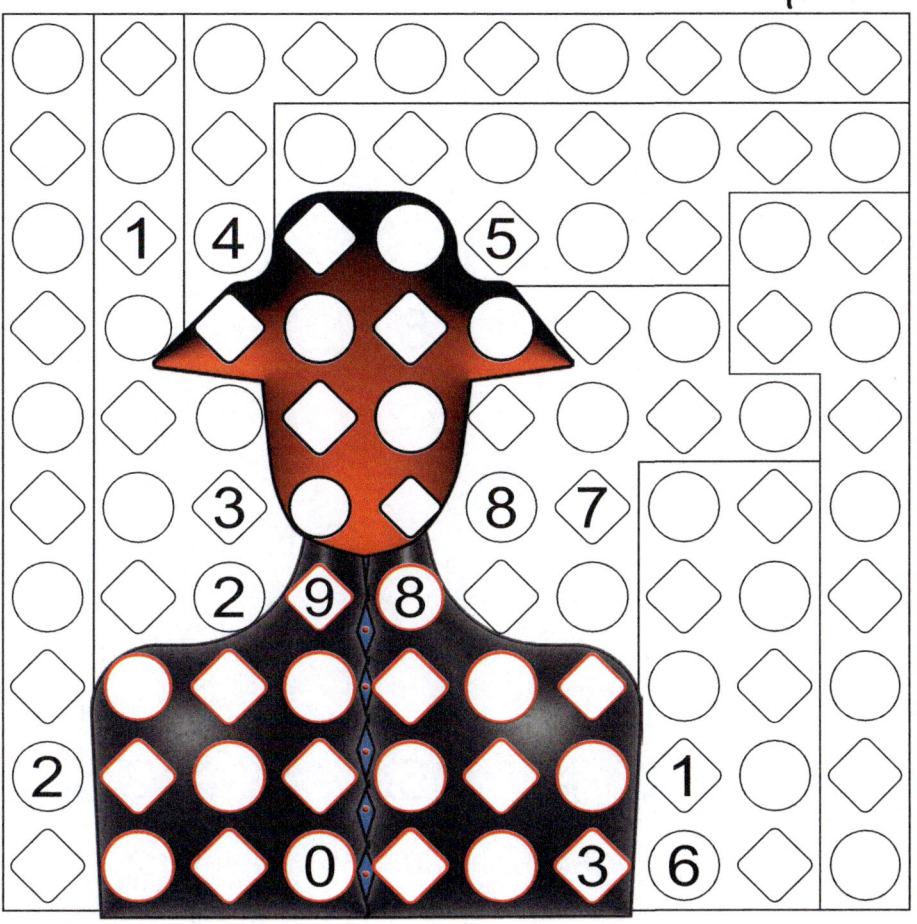

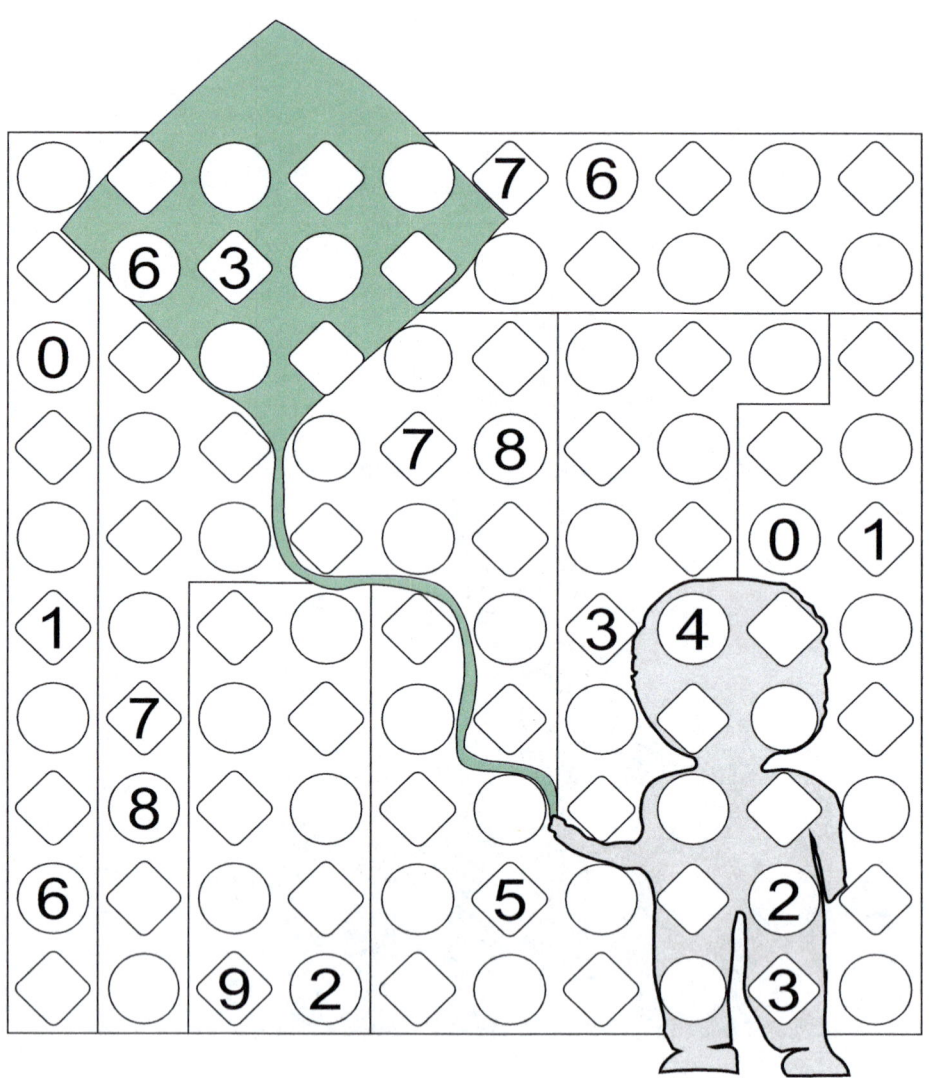

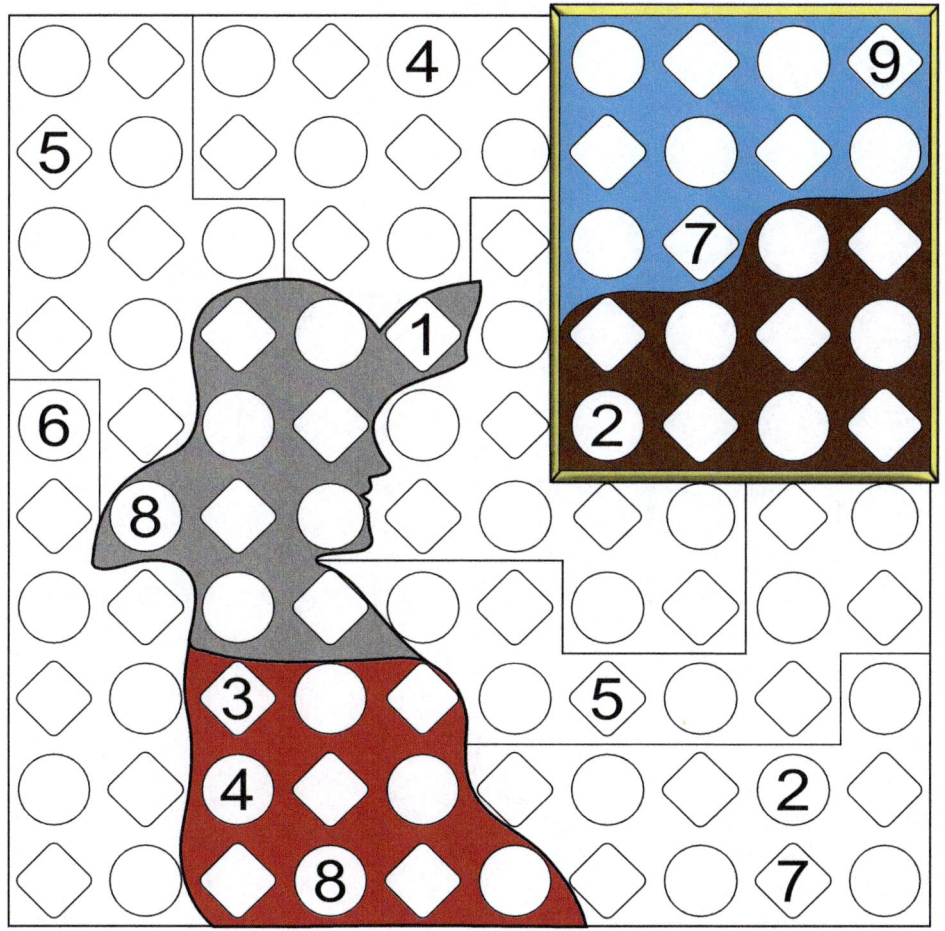

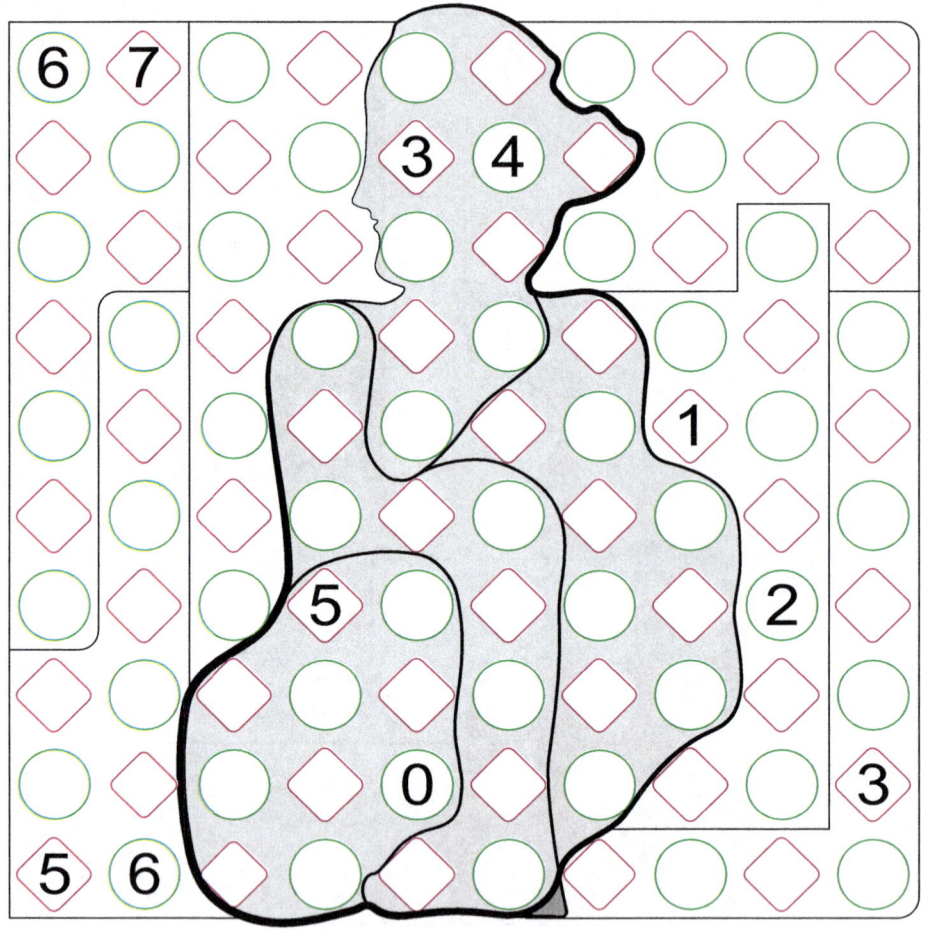

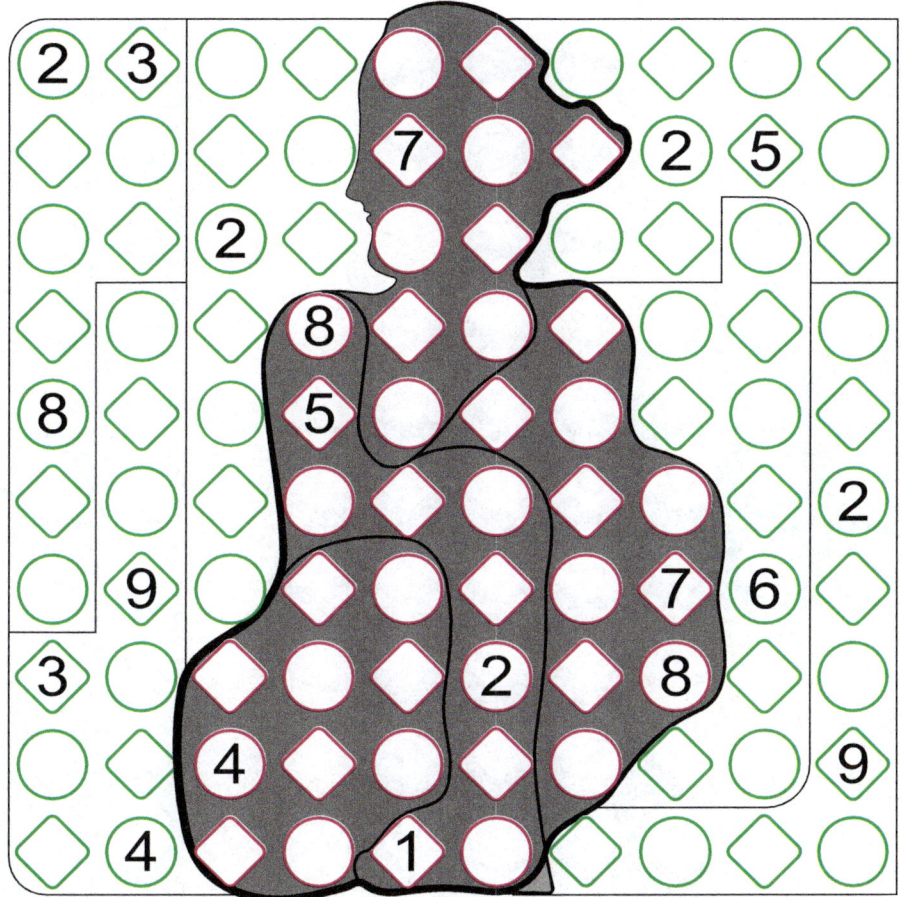

53

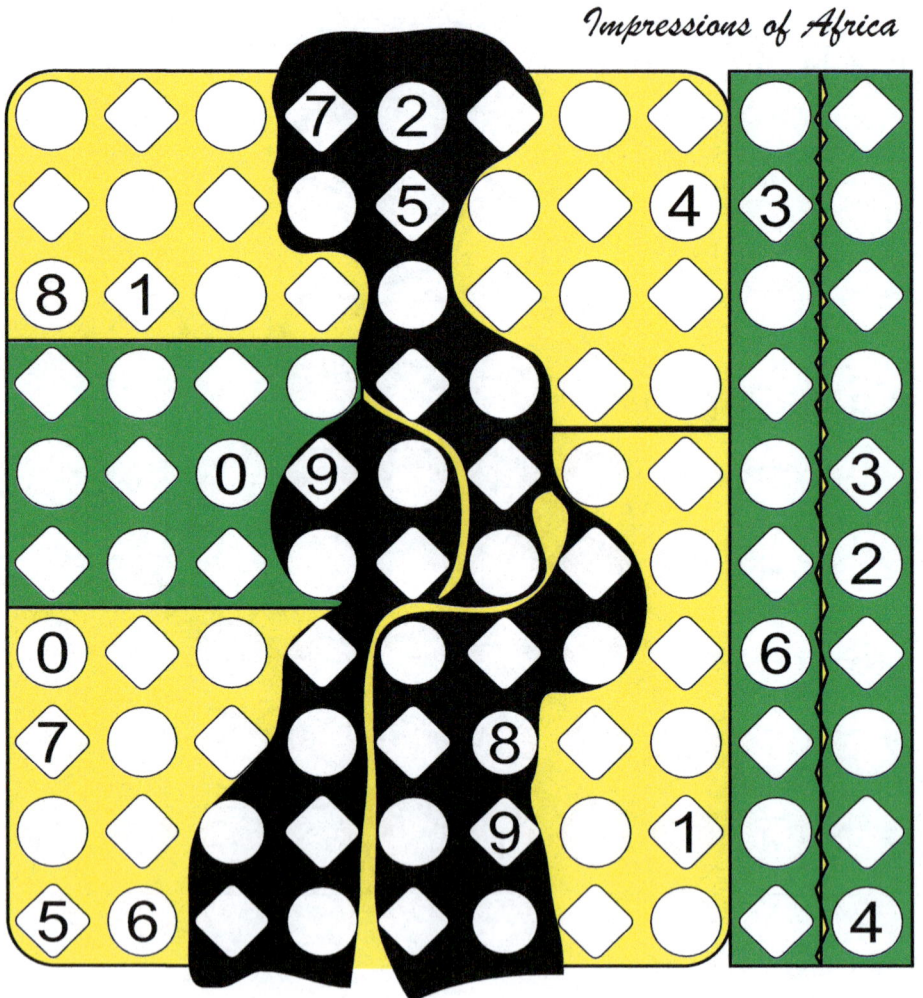

*Impressions of Africa*

# The Shadow Deal

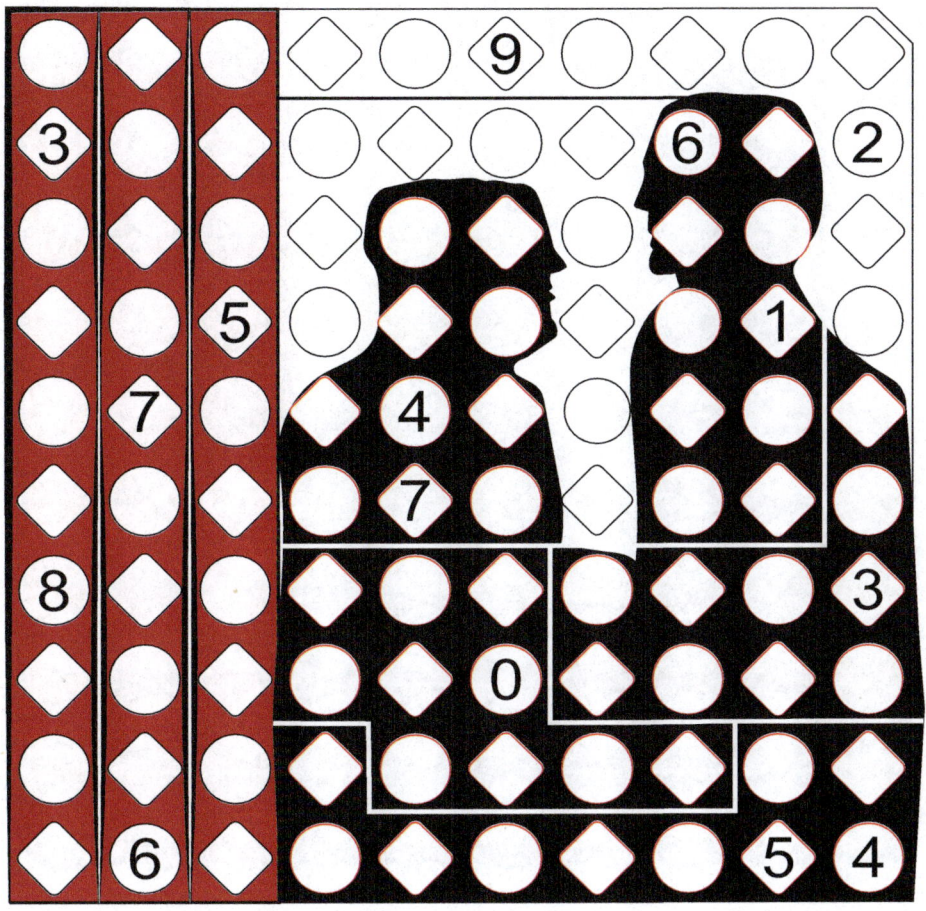

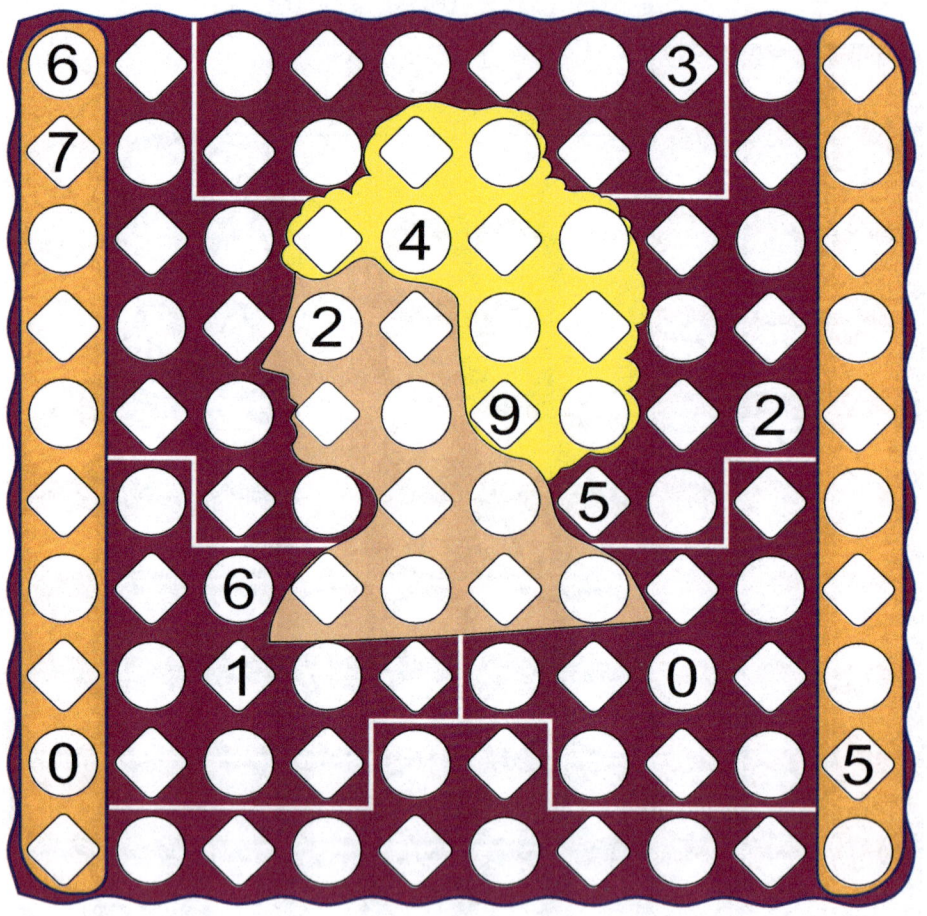

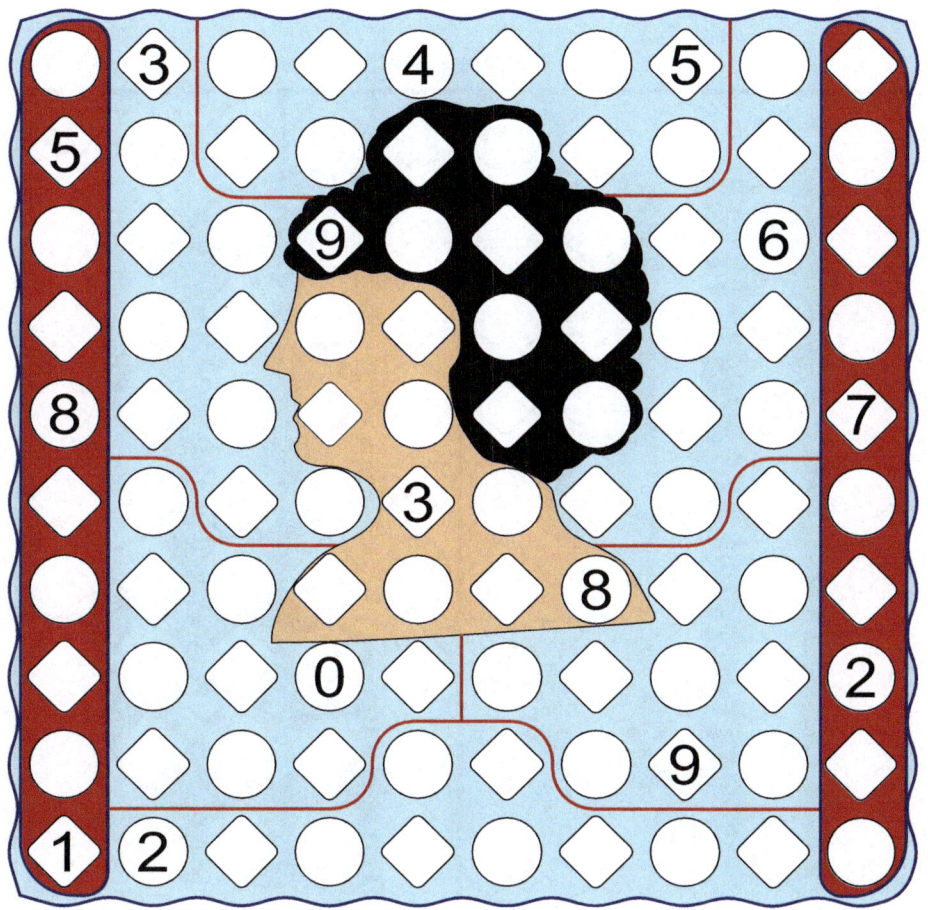

**The Appraisal**

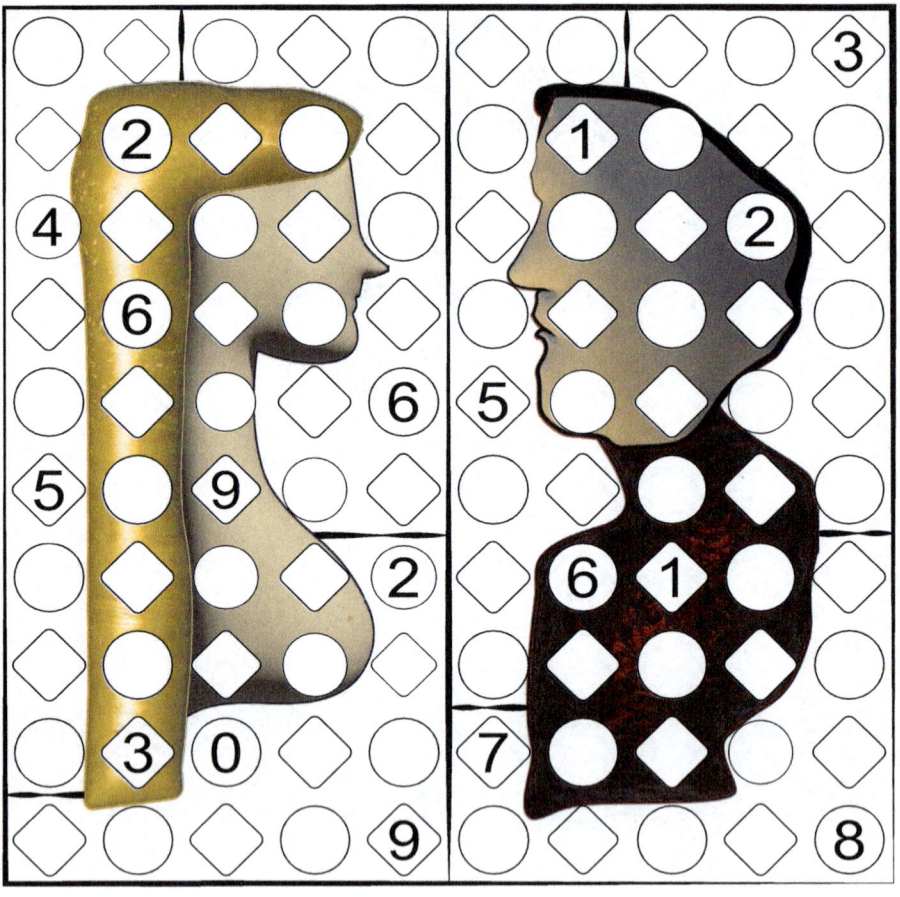

58

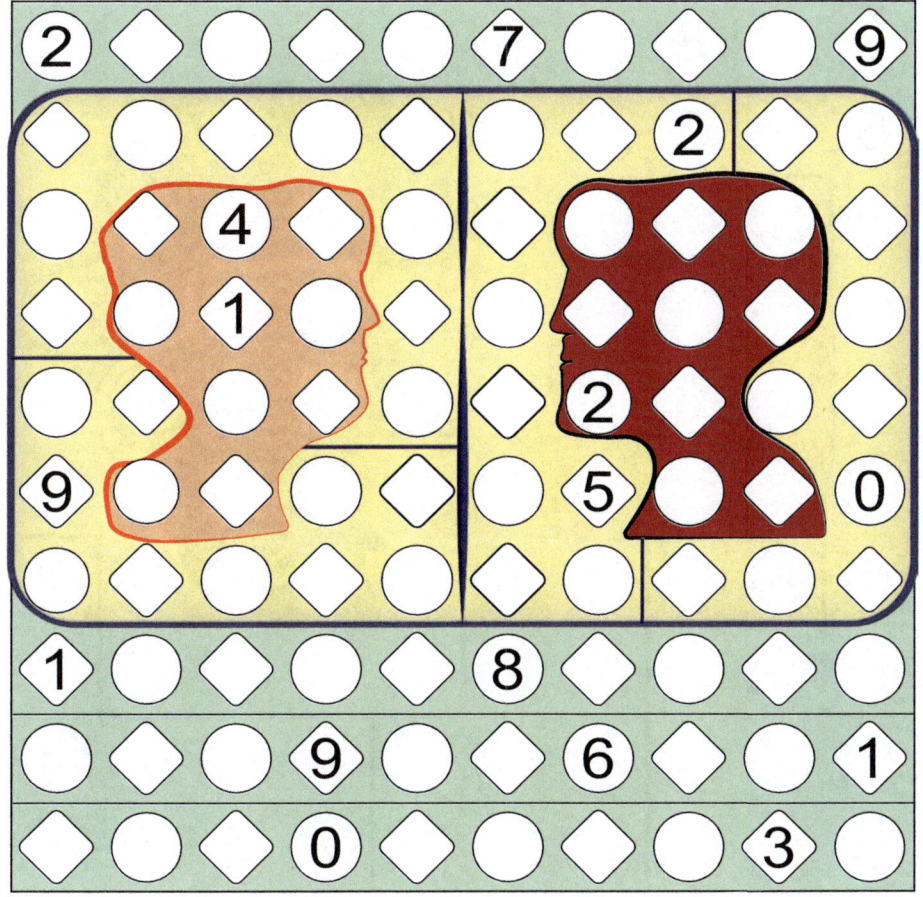

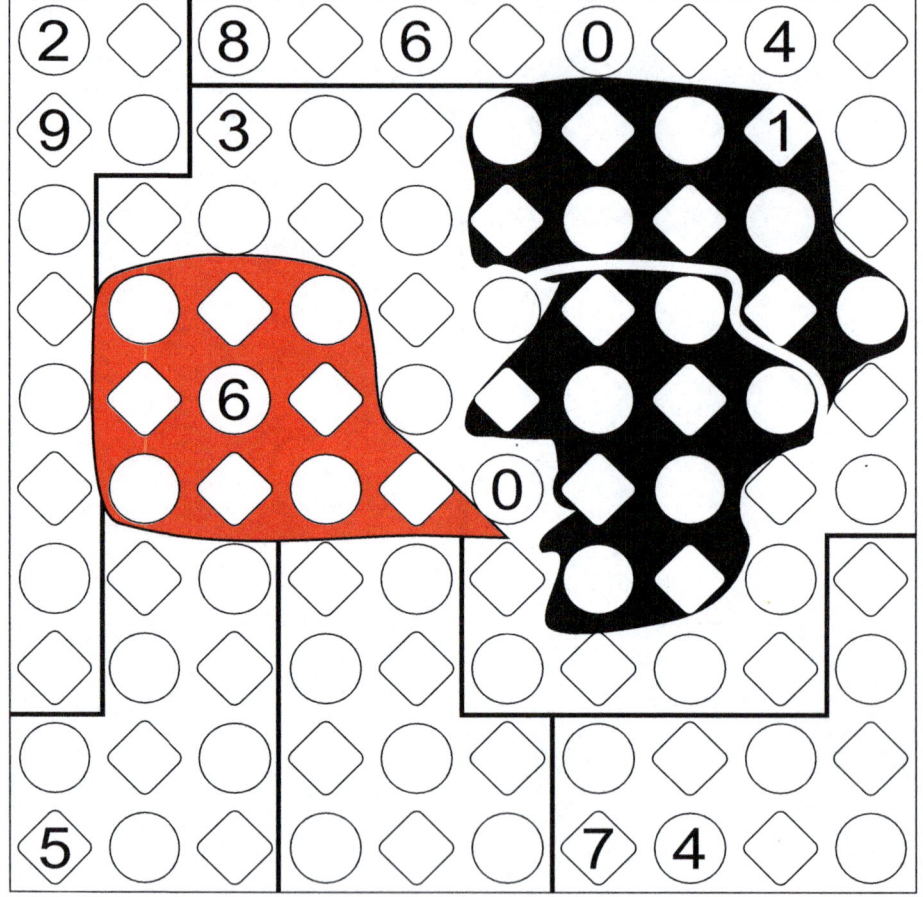

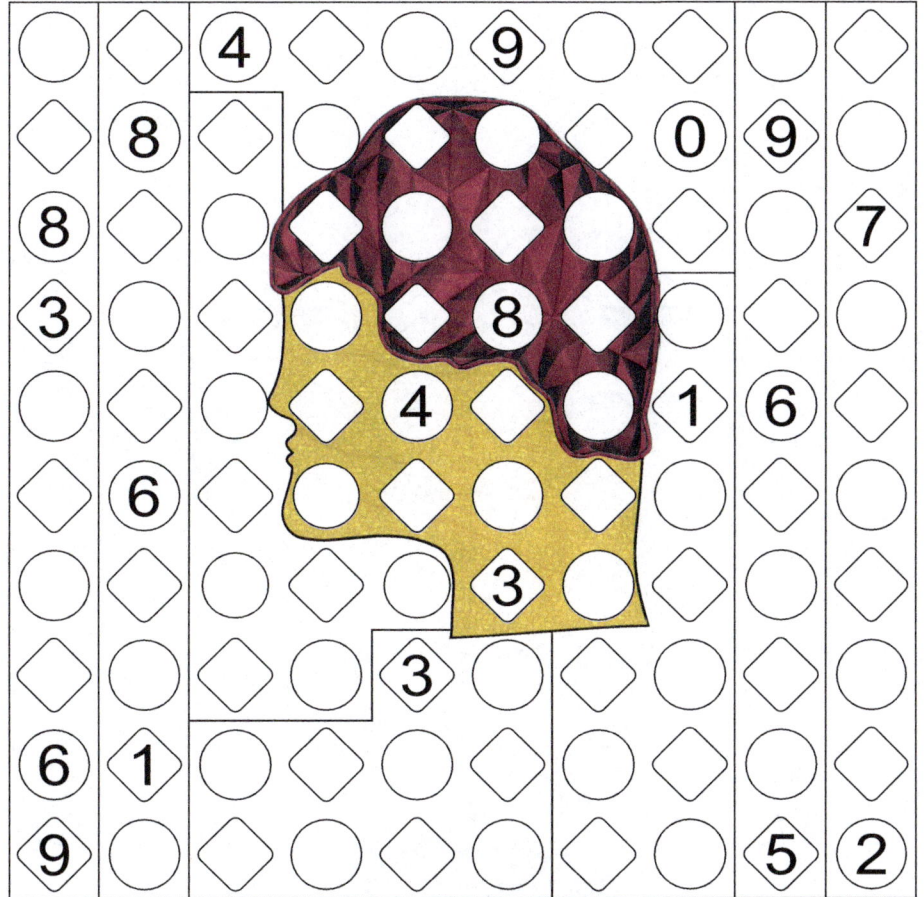

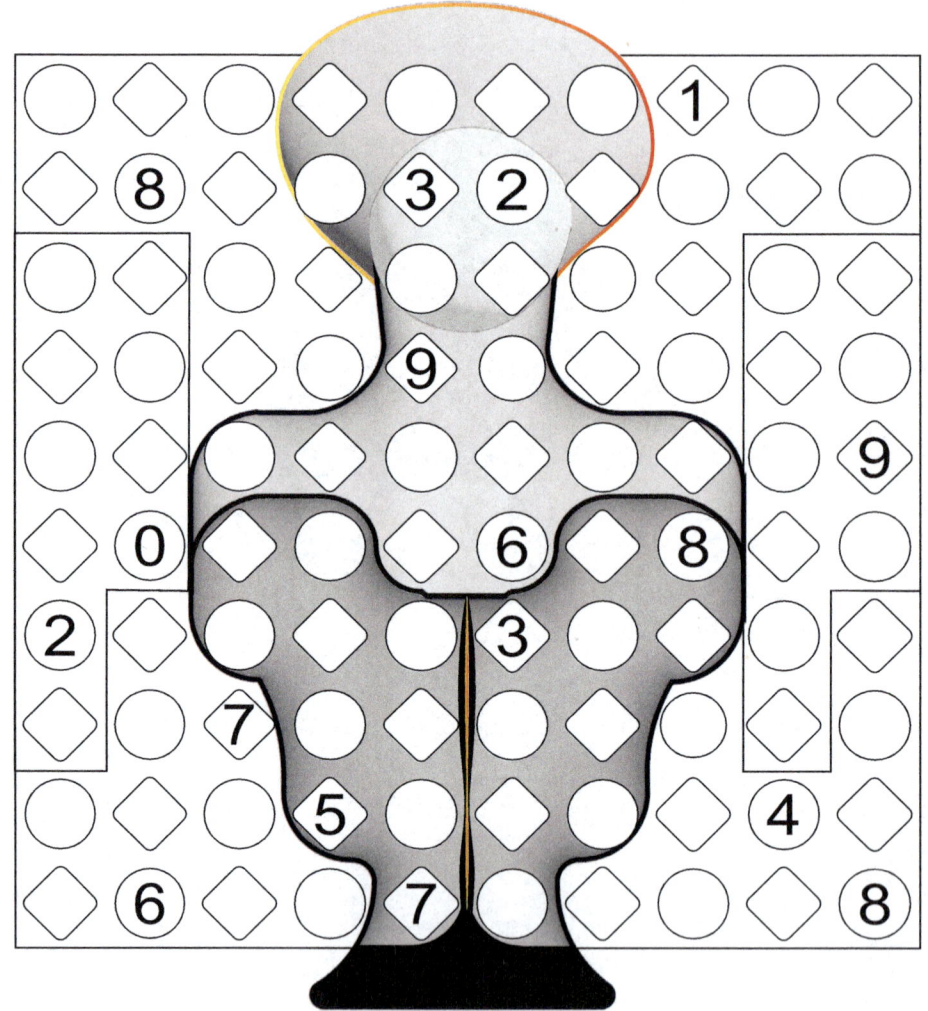

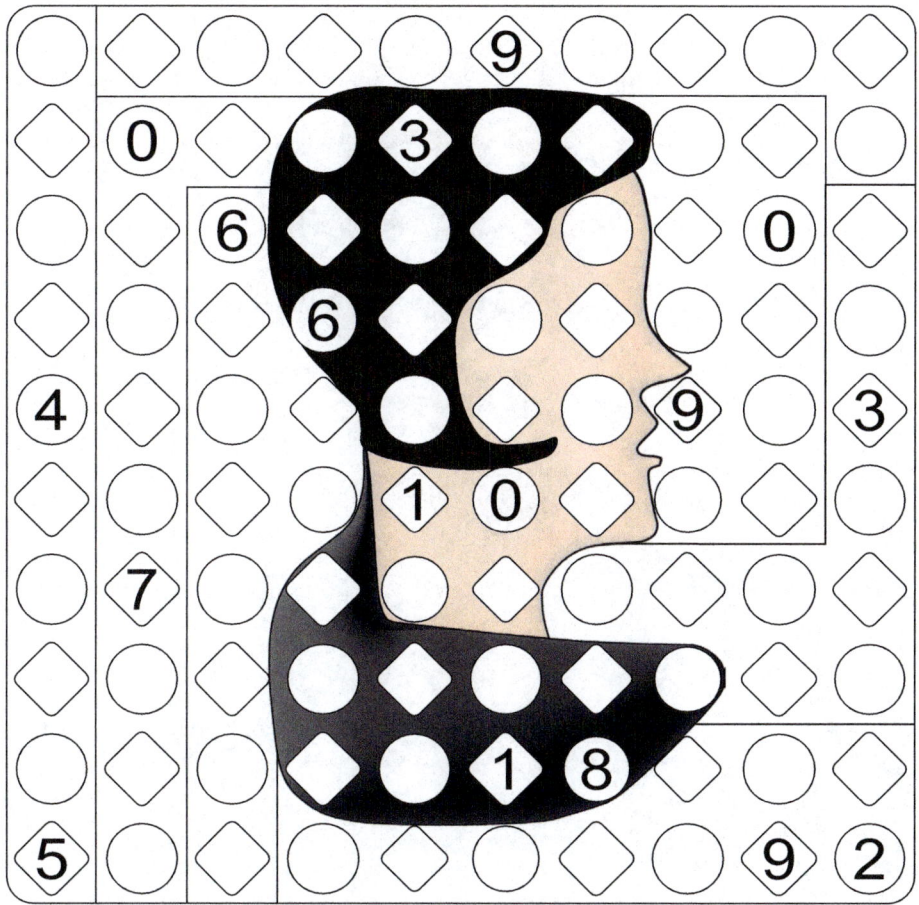

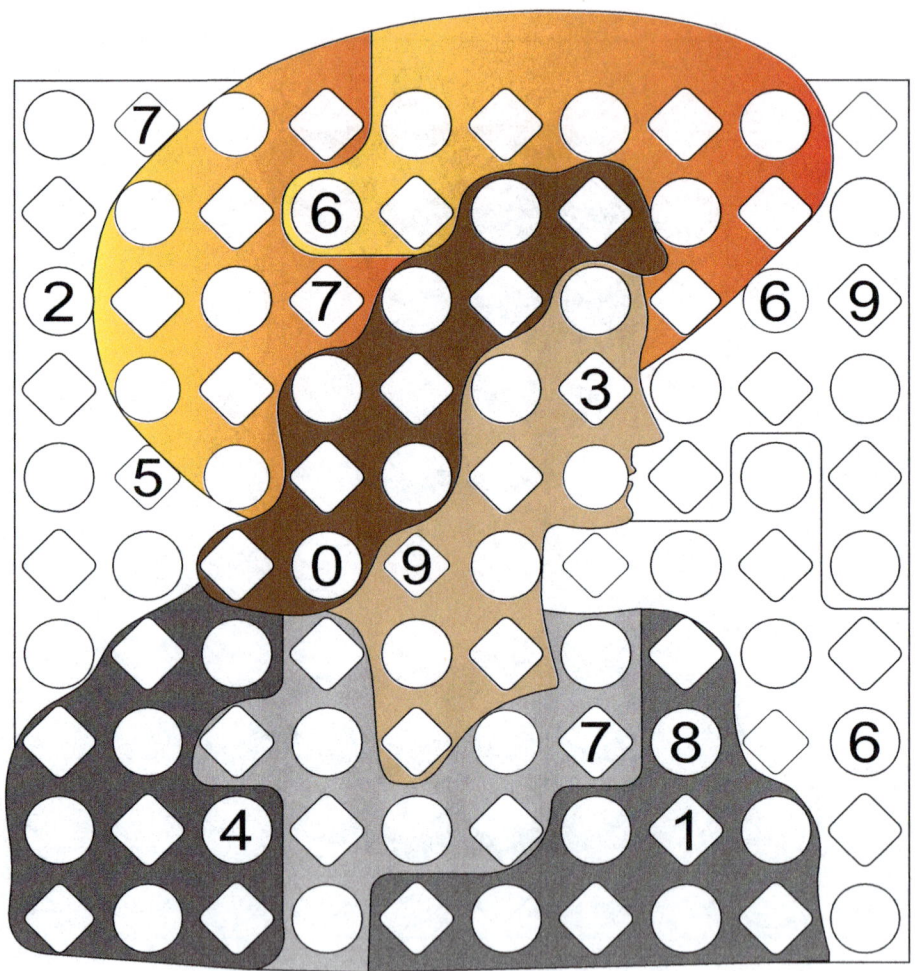

The Vision

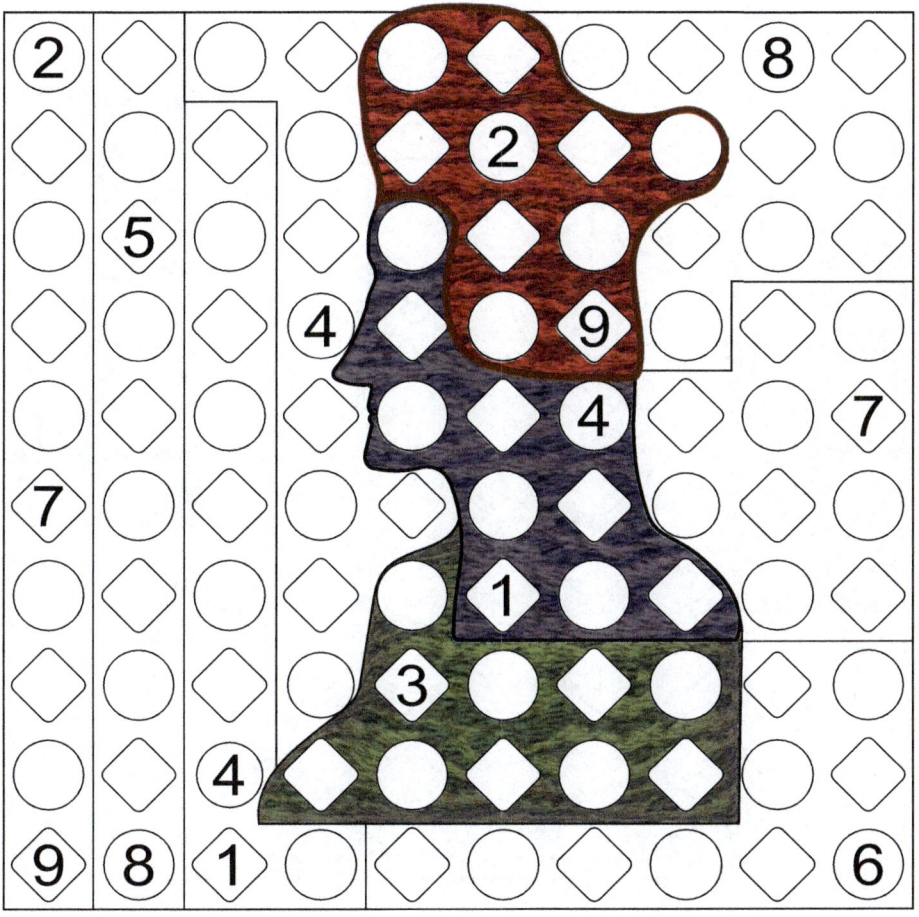

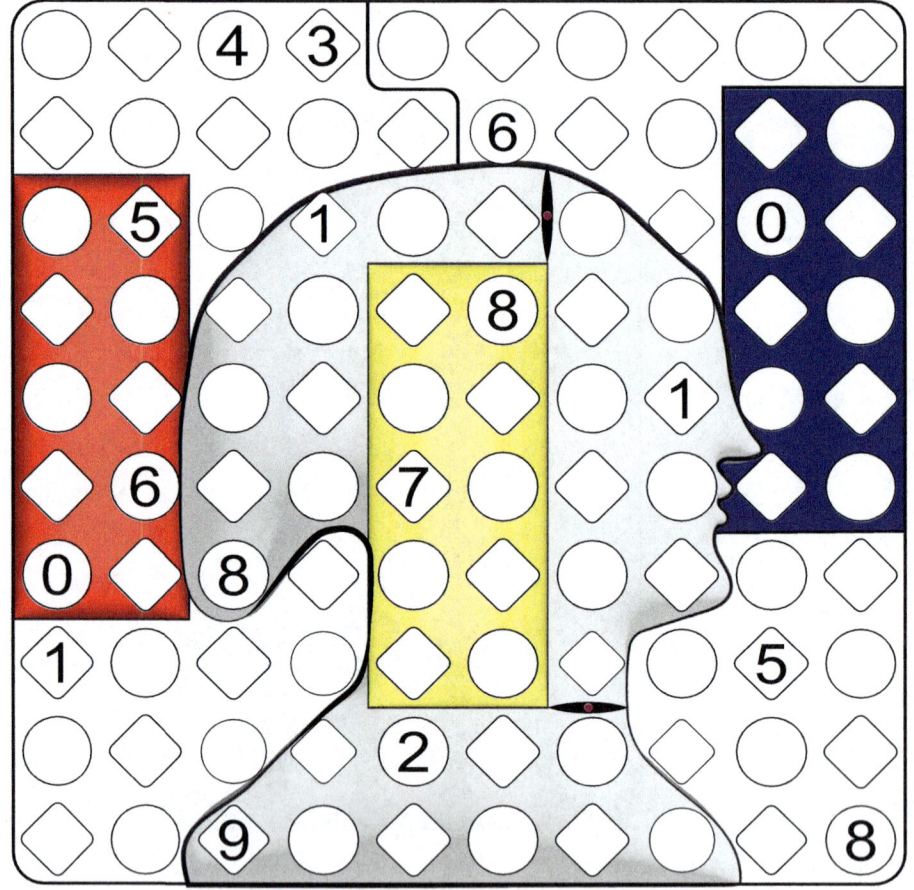

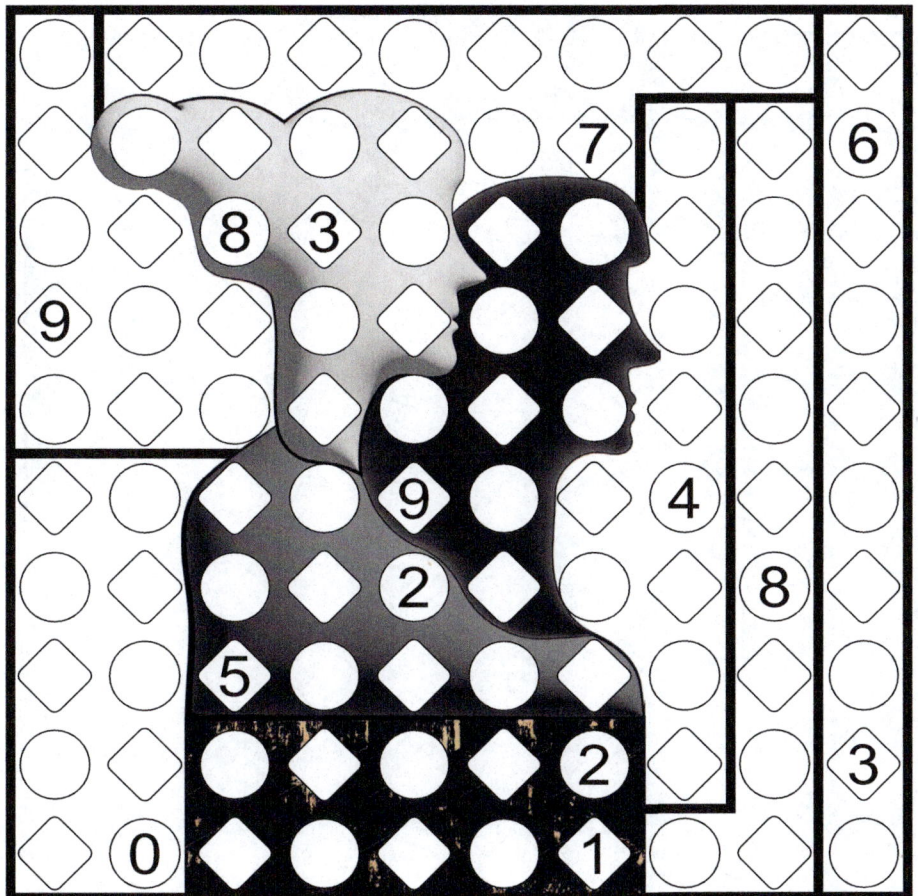

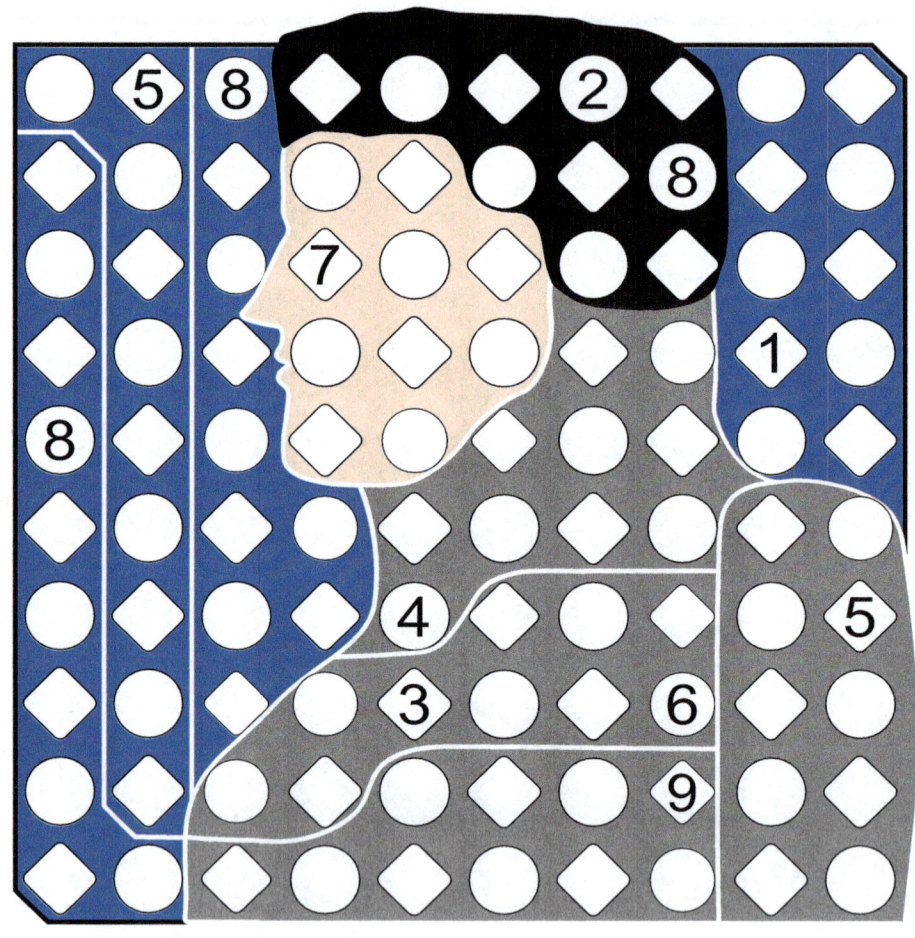

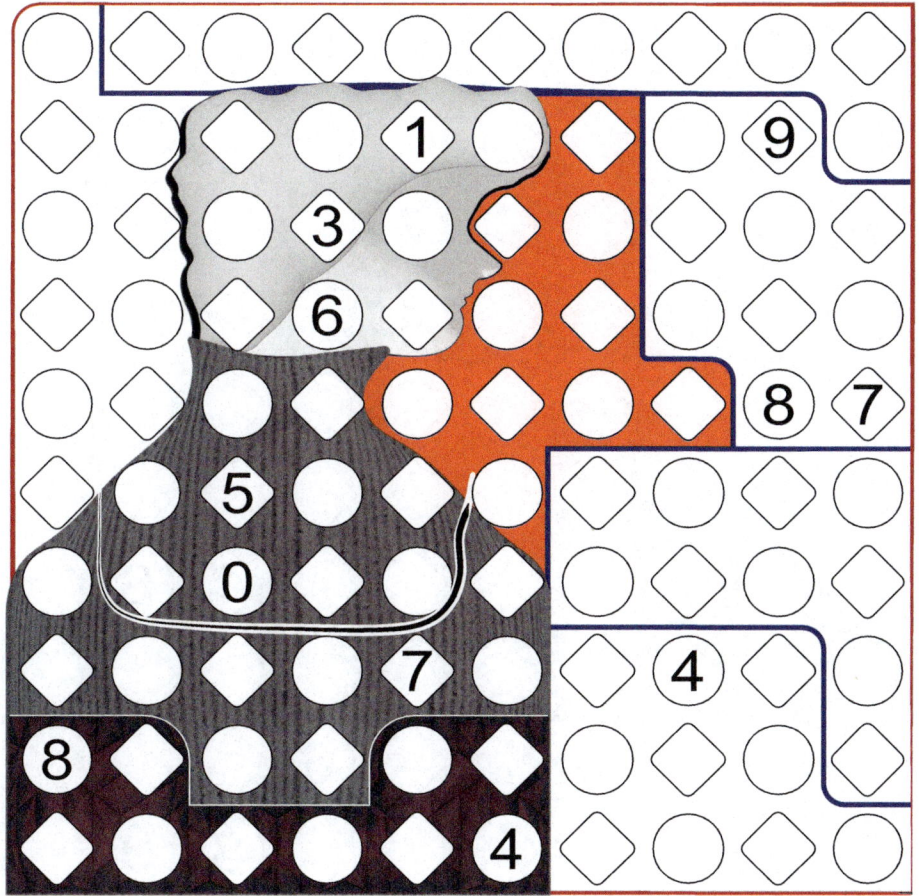

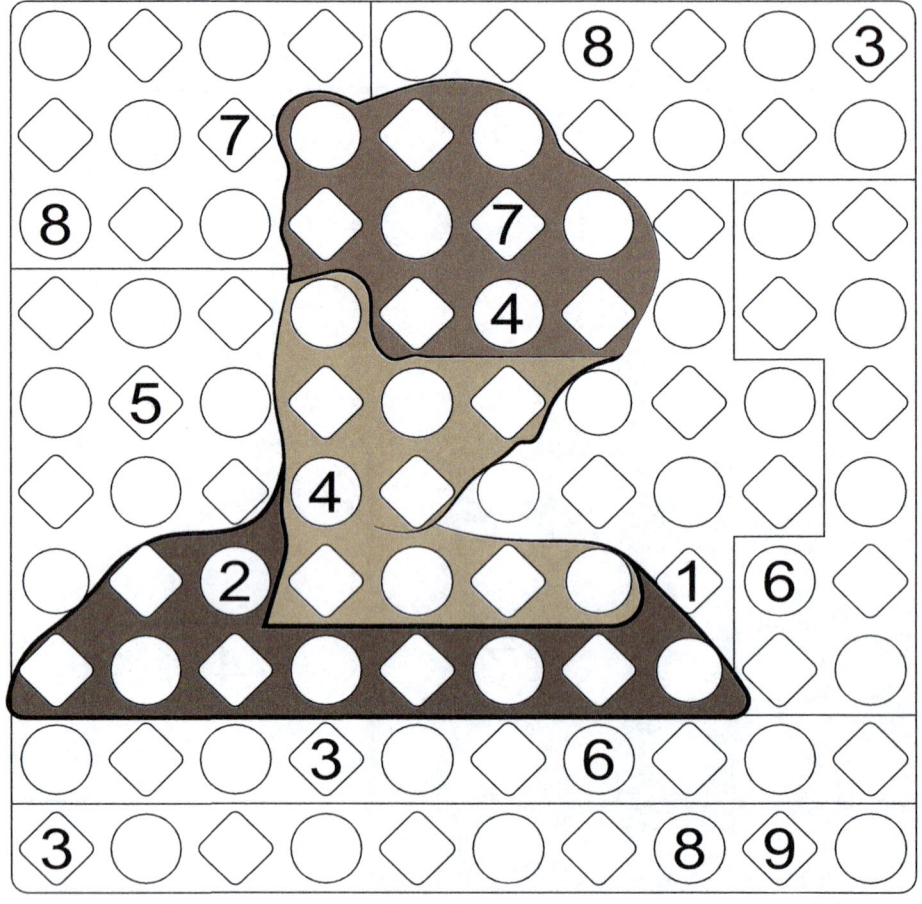

70

# The Crime Scene

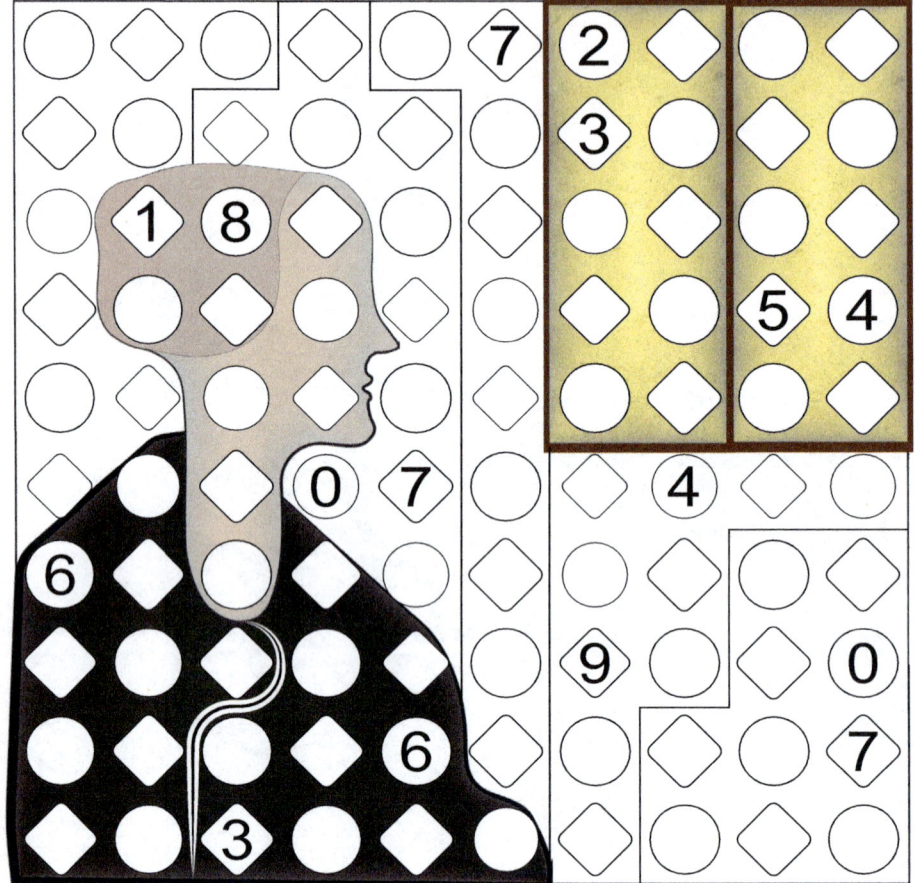

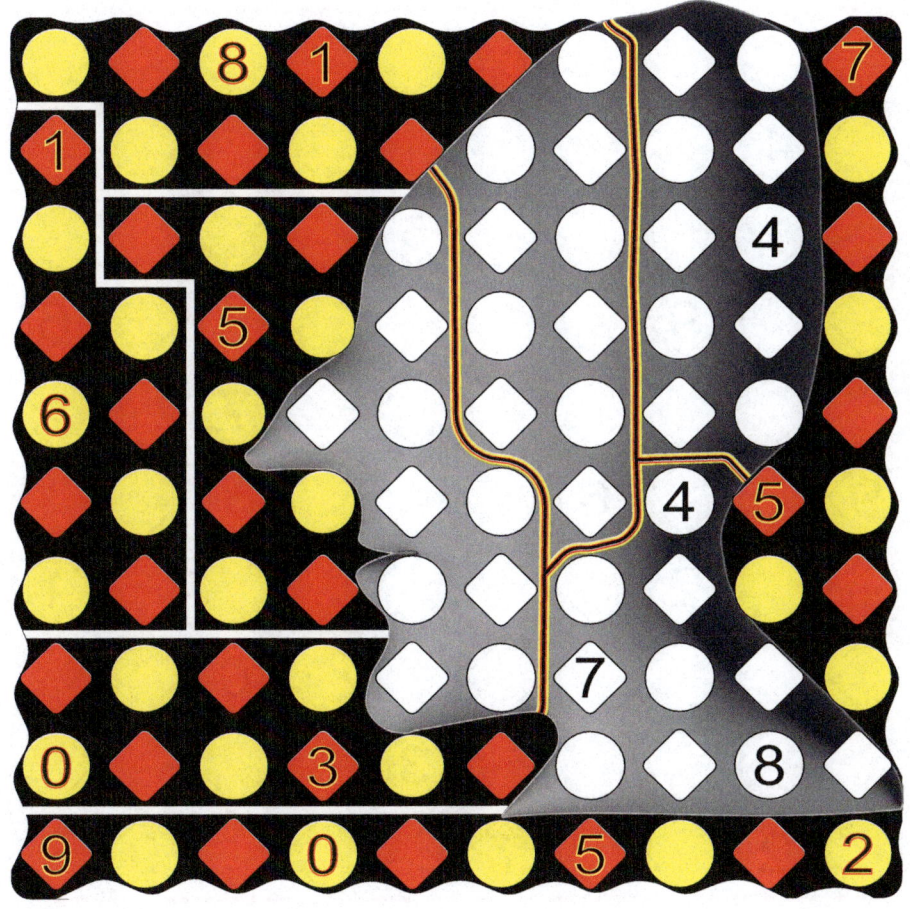

73

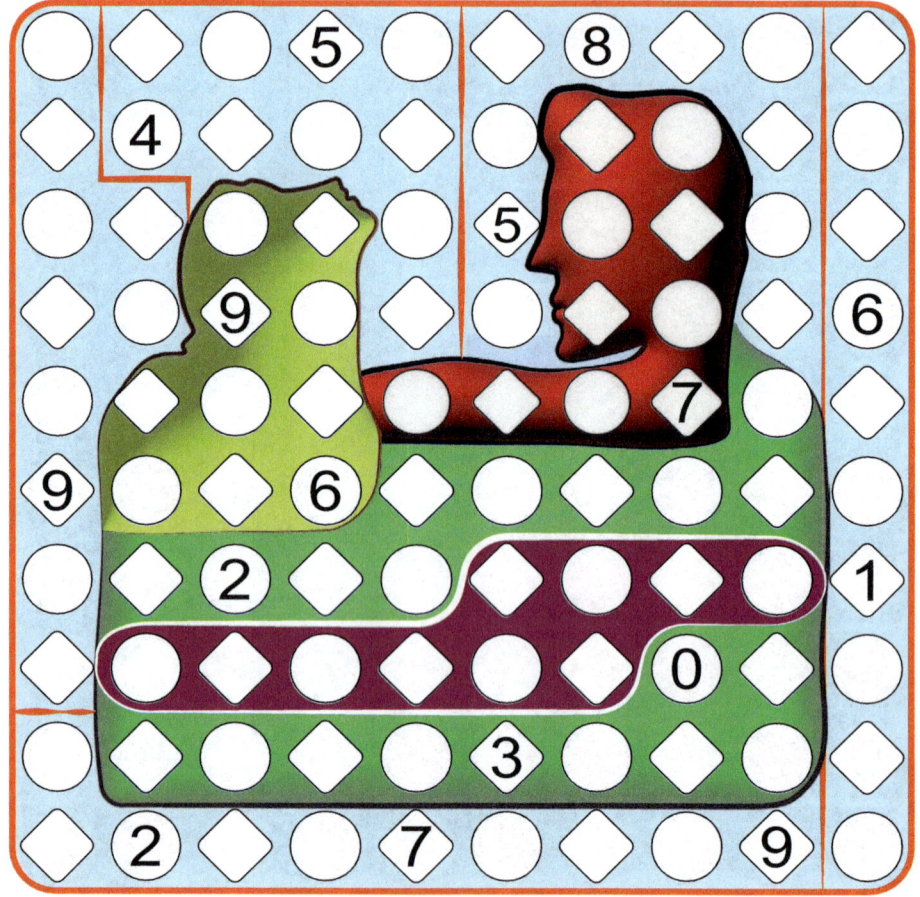

# Solutions

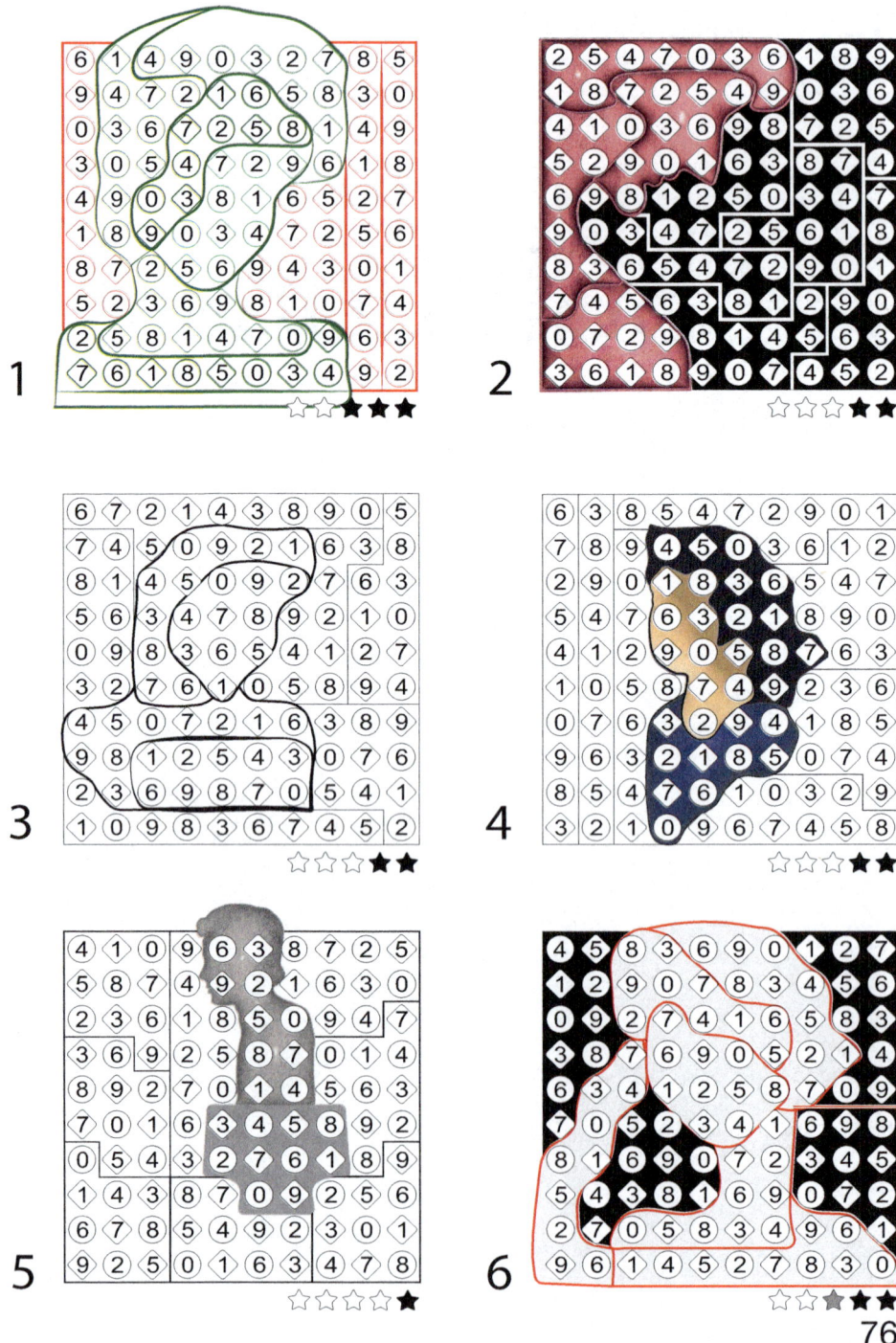

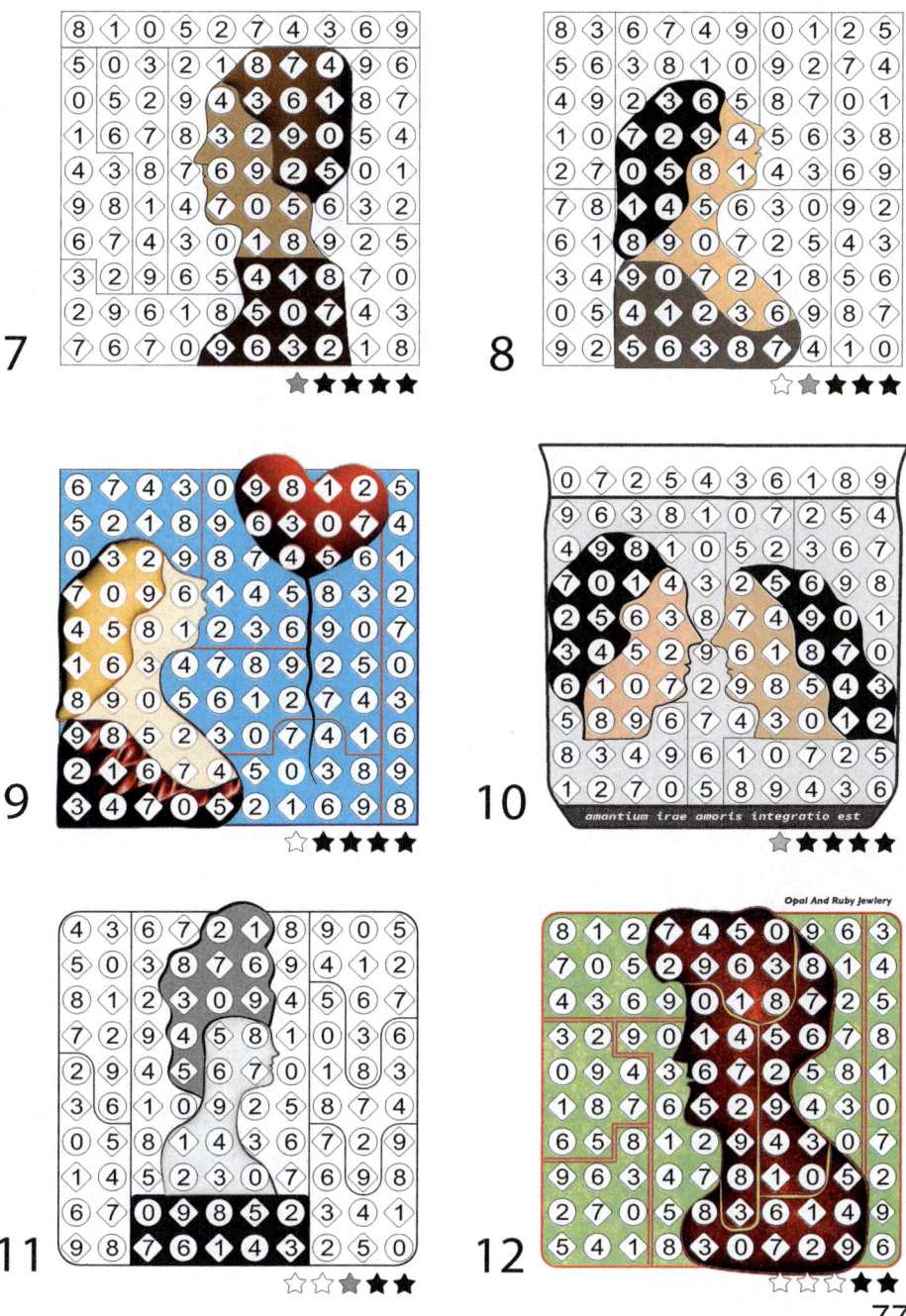

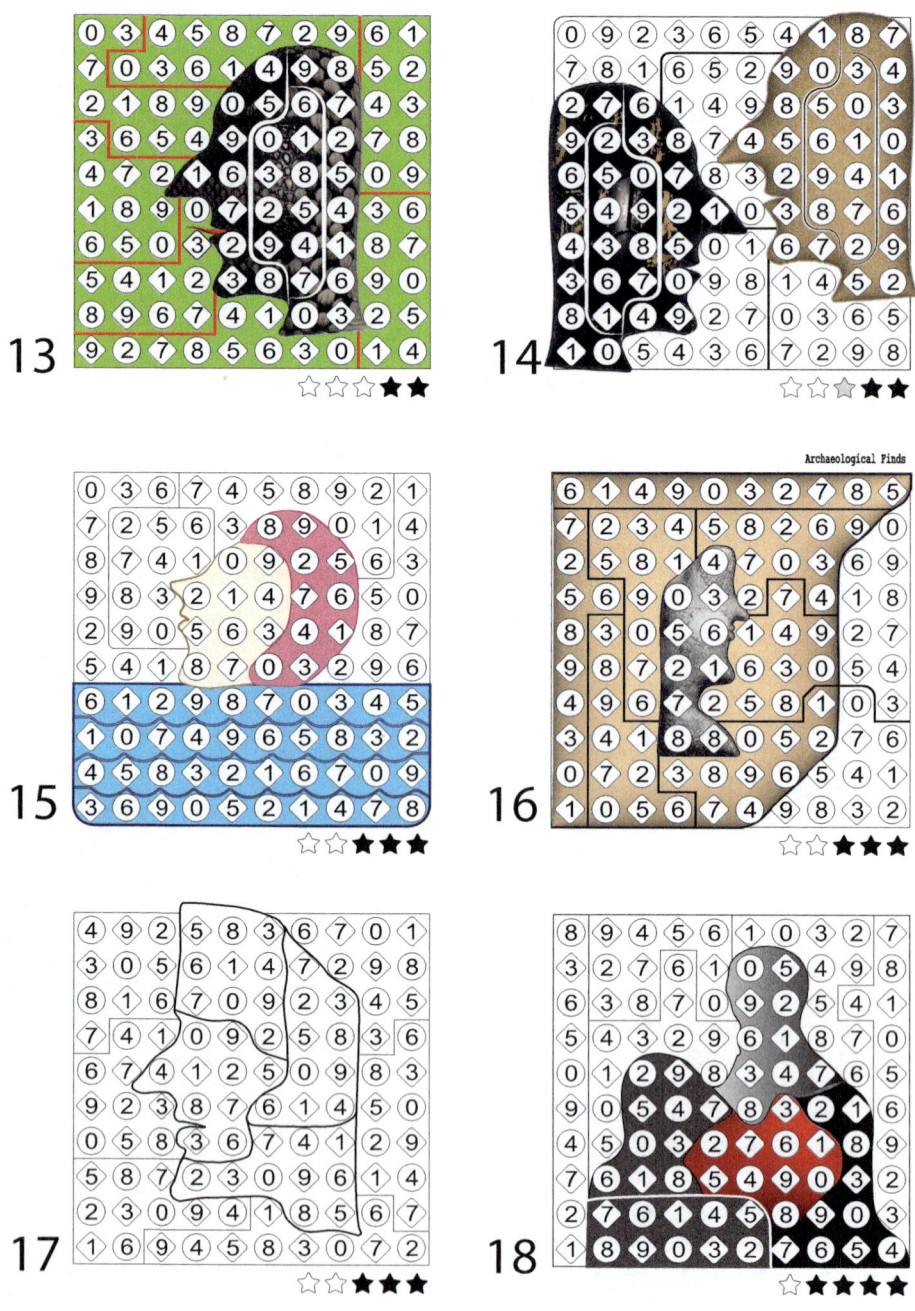

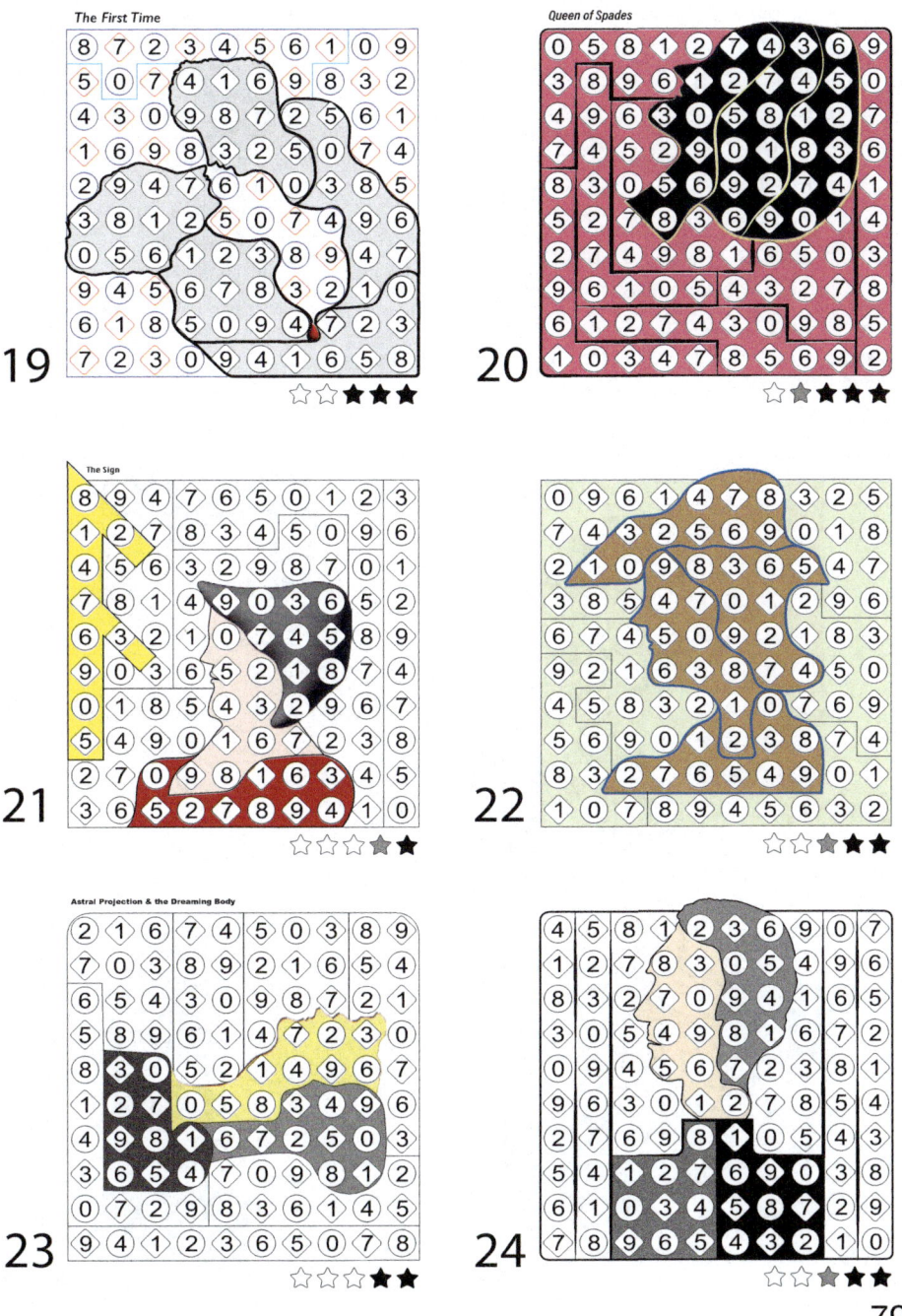

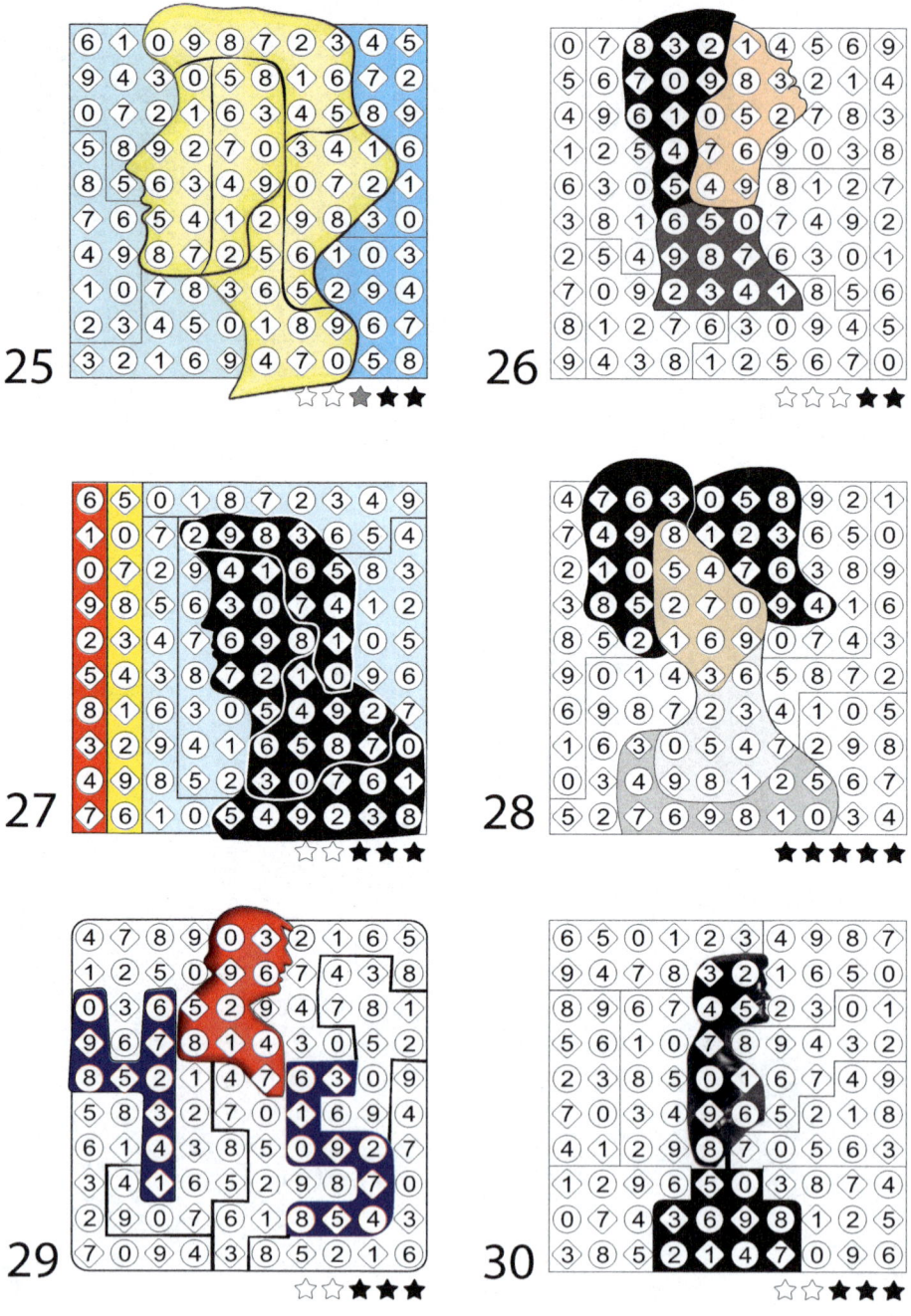

80

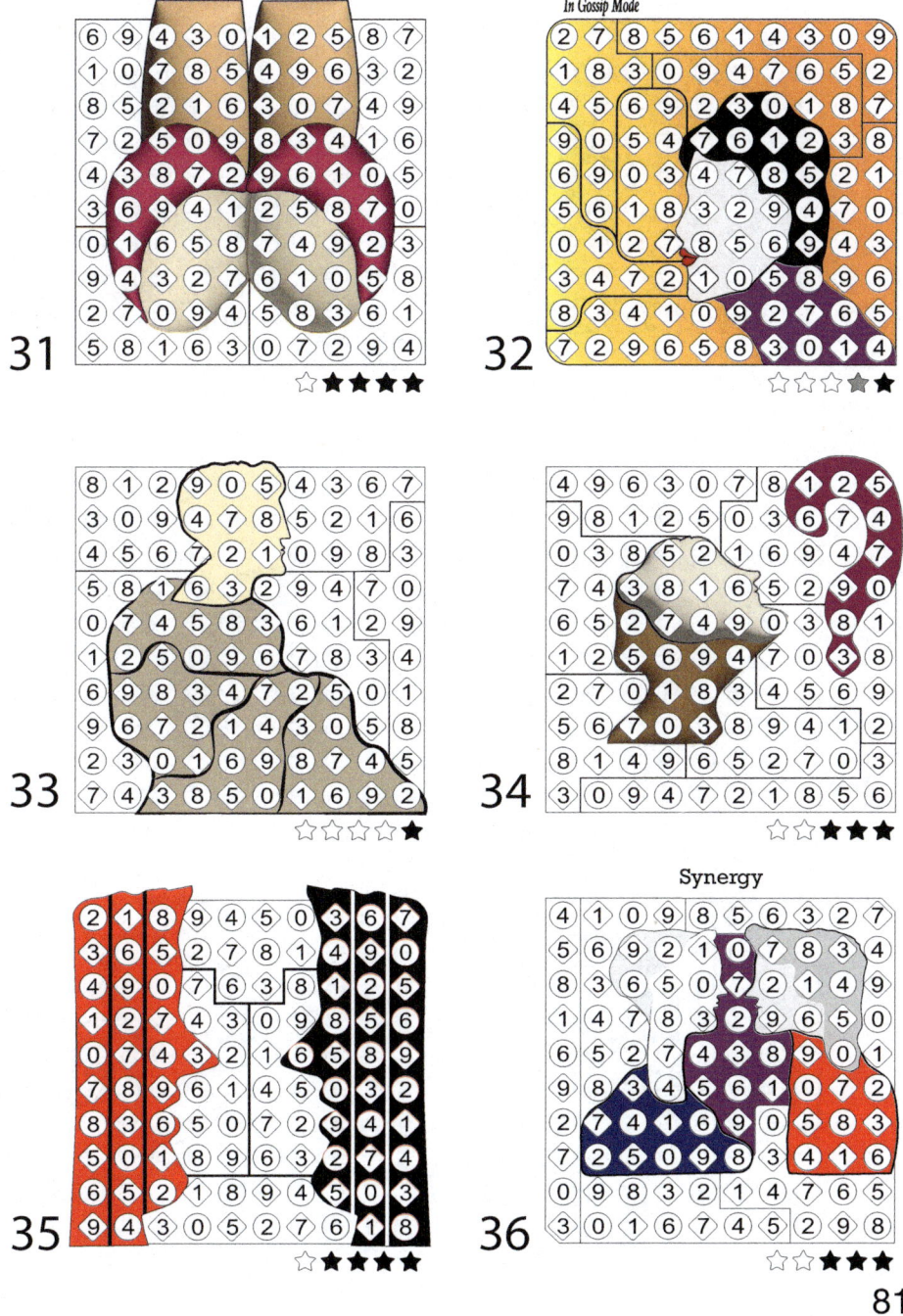

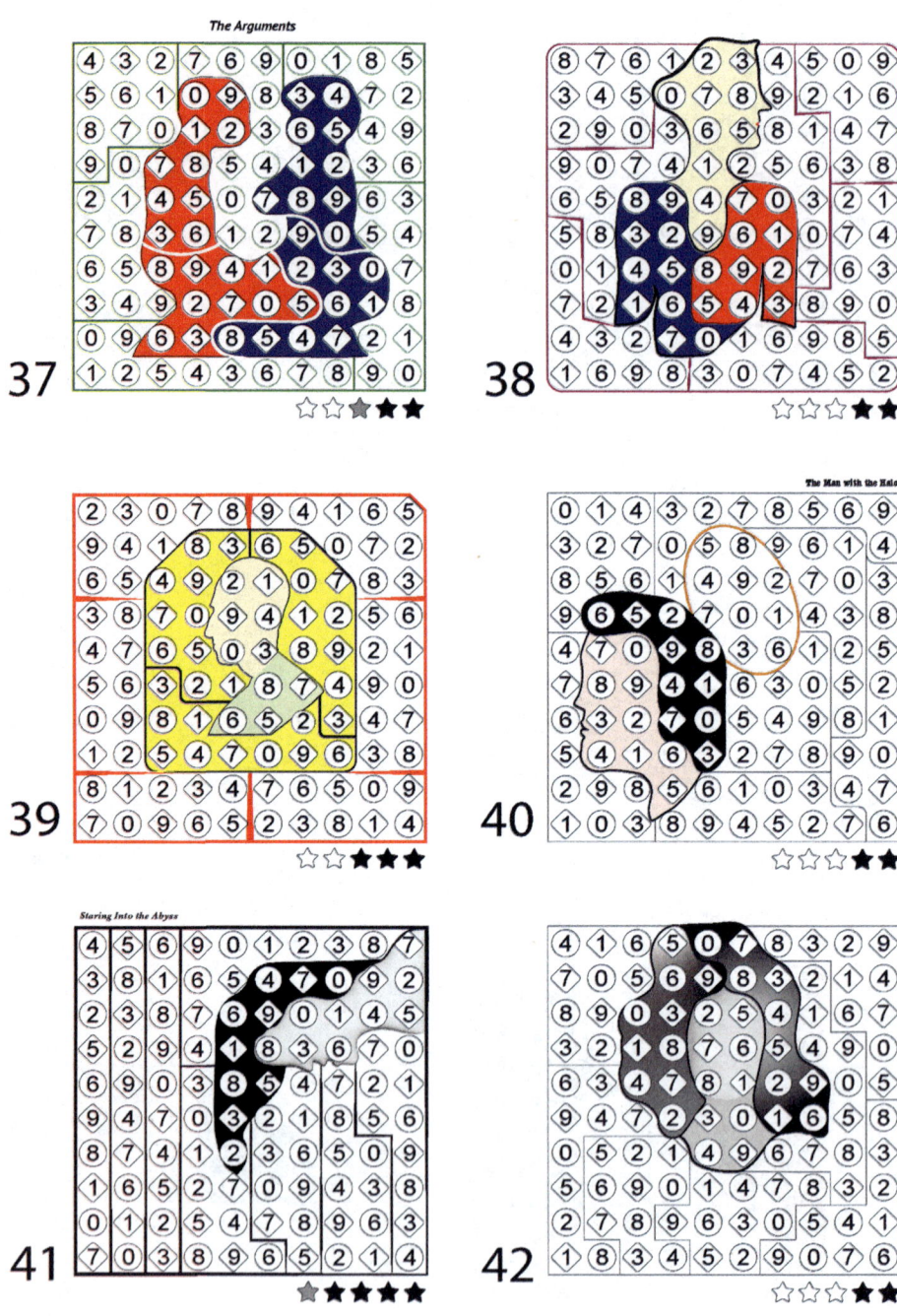

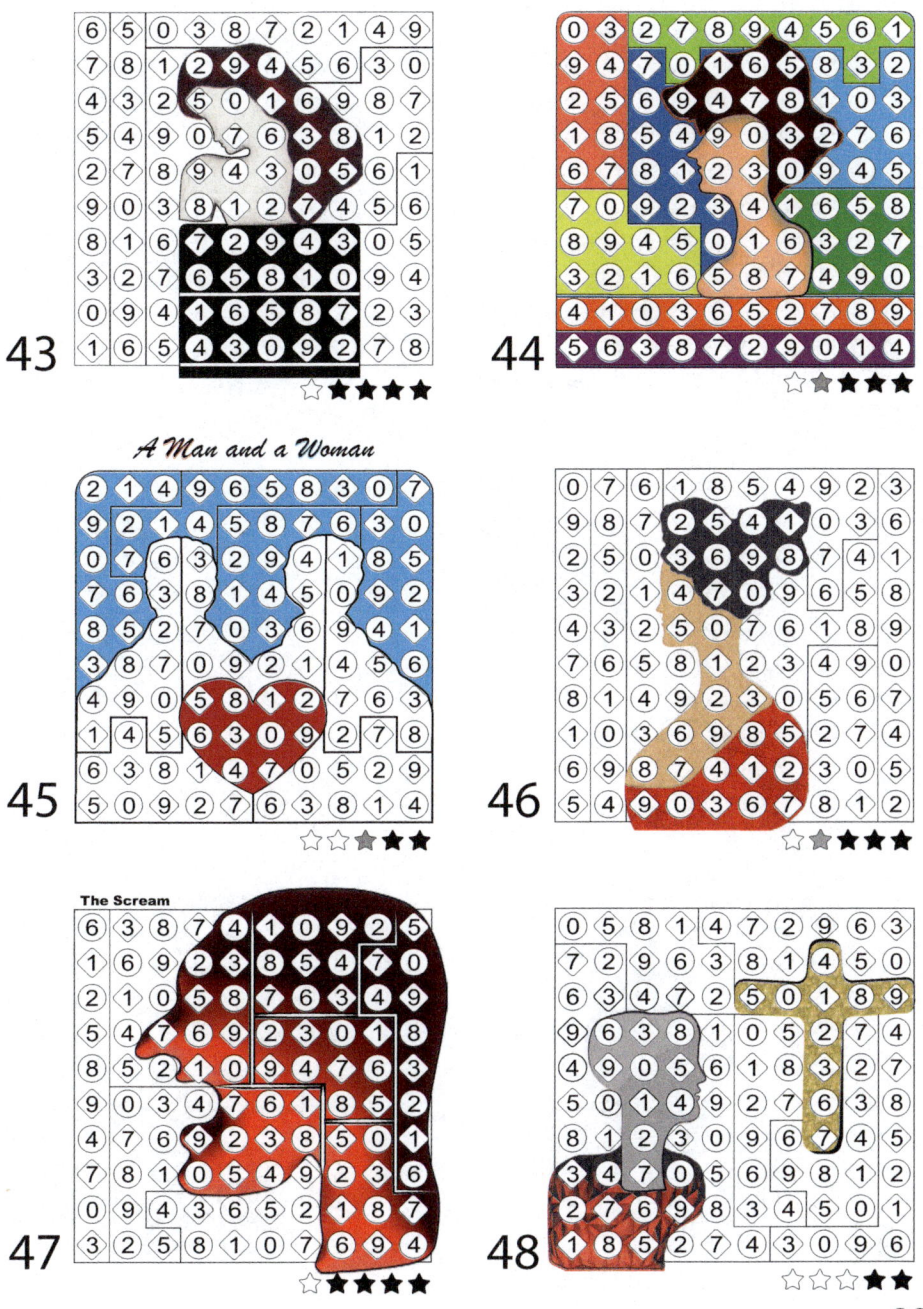

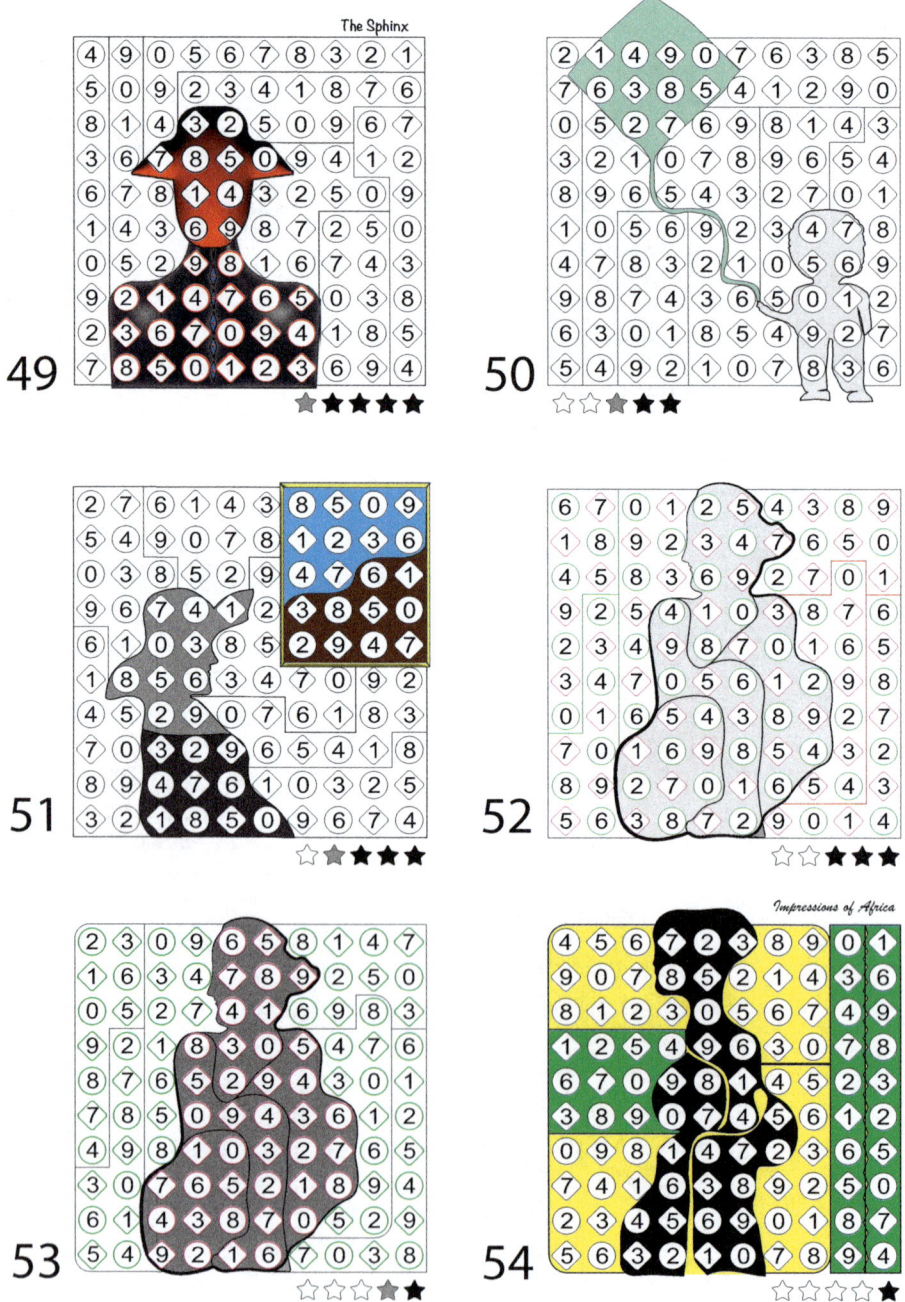

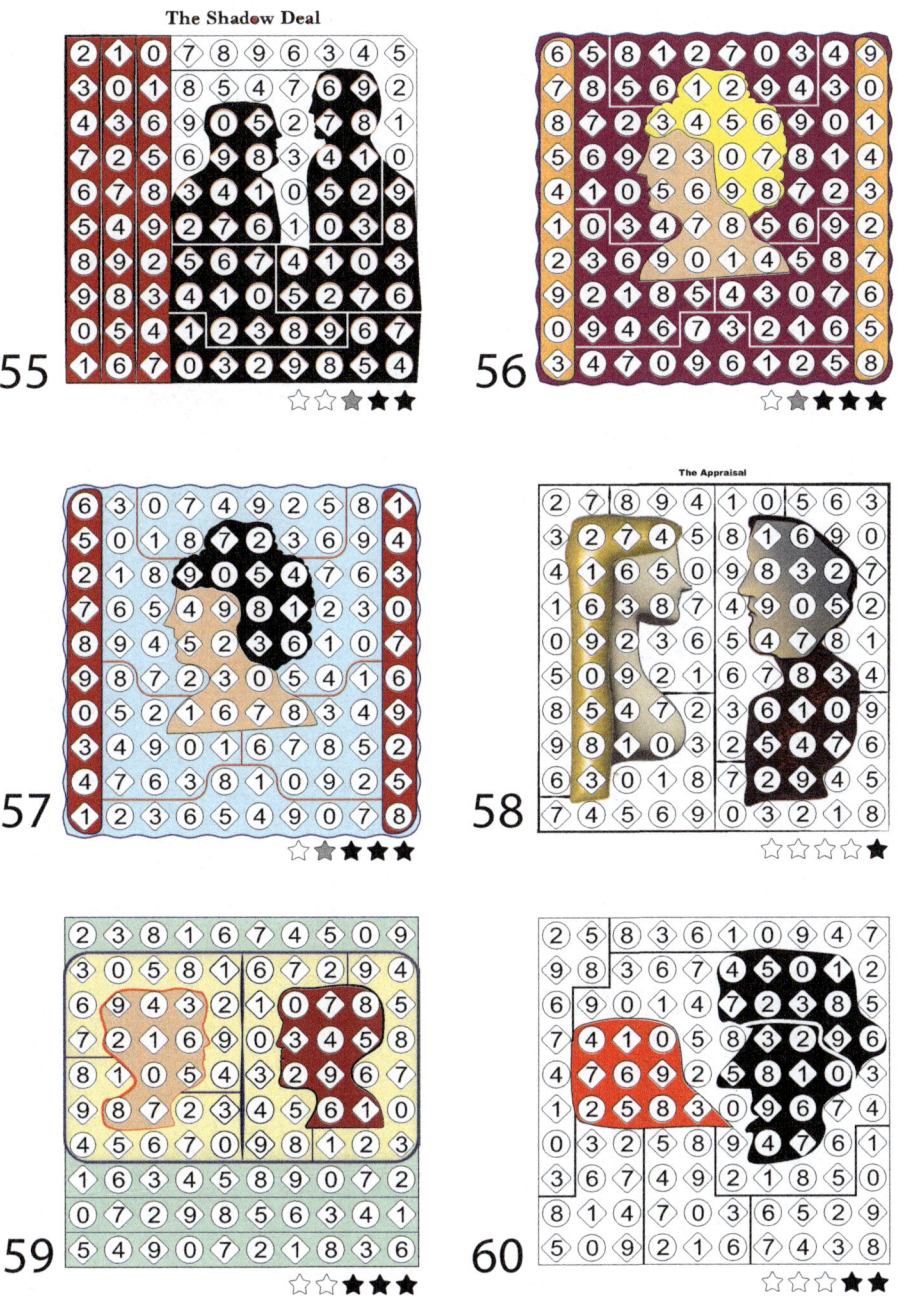

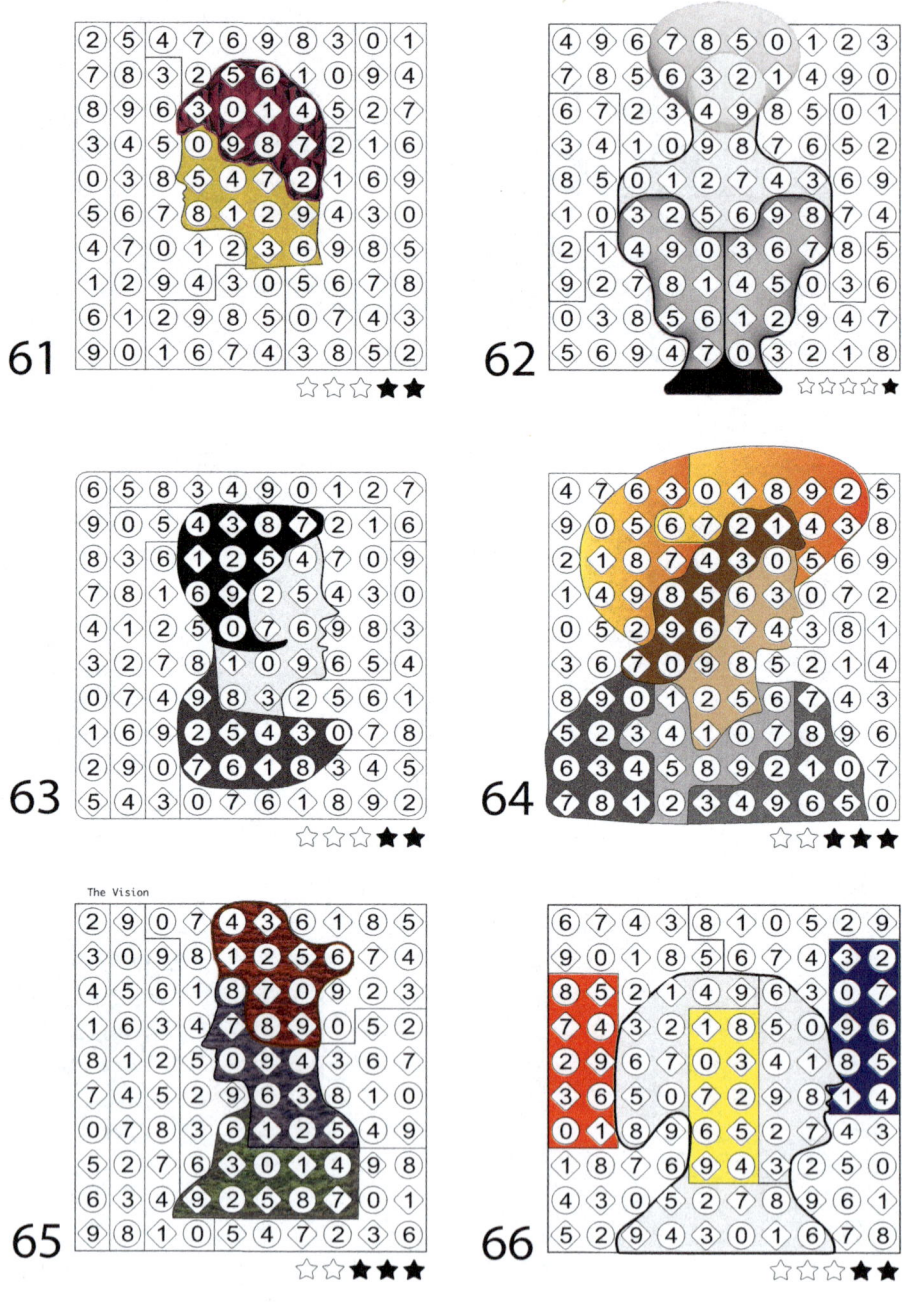

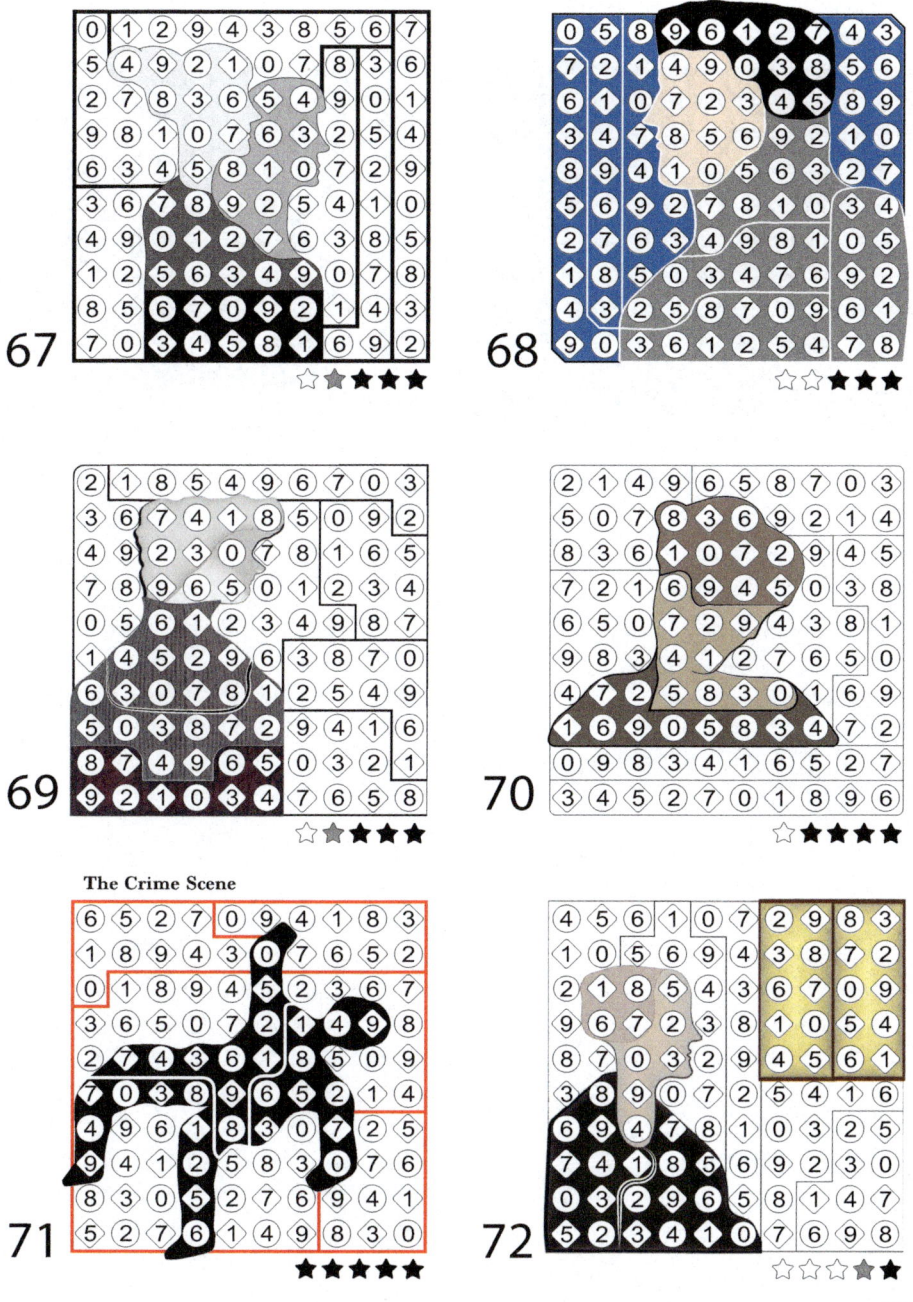

73 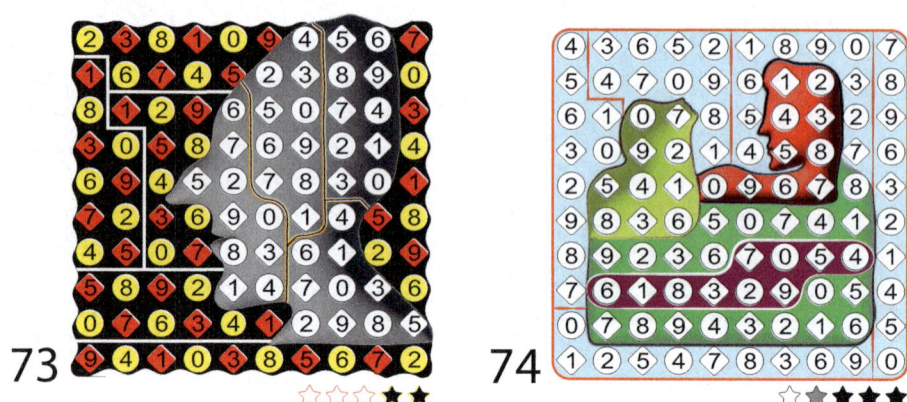 74

Printed in Dunstable, United Kingdom